The

Endangered

American

Dream

Other books by Timothy Robert Walters:

Surviving the Second Civil War: the Land Rights Battle . . . and How To Win It

From My Cold Dead Fingers: Why America Needs Guns!*

Government, GOD and Freedom: A Fundamental Trinity*

Judevar (western fiction)**

*Co-authored by Richard I. Mack
**Originally published by Sunstone Press

All titles available through Rawhide Western Publishing (see back pages).

The Endangered American Dream

Land Lock—the Cancer That's Killing America . . . and How To Stop It!

Timothy Robert Walters

RAWHIDE WESTERN PUBLISHING

P.O. Box 327 . 4753 S. 16th Lane . Safford, AZ 85548

First Edition: Published by Rawhide Western Publishing, Dec. 1995.
Cover design by Renee Anthony Agency.

Typeset in Times New Roman on Intel computers by Rawhide Western
Publishing, PO Box 327, Safford, Arizona 85548-0327.
Telephone 520-428-5956. Fax 520-428-7010.

Printing and Perfectbind by Griffin Printing, 4141 N. Freeway Blvd.,
Sacramento, California 95834. 916-649-3511.

Conceived and produced in the United States of America . . . the Land
of Freedom and Unalienable Rights.

———————————————————

Walters, Timothy Robert, 1945
        The endangered American dream : land lock—the
    cancer that's killing America . . . and how to stop it!
America / Timothy Robert Walters. — 1st ed.

        Includes bibliographic references and index.

        ISBN 0-9641935-3-1 : $16.95

        Library of Congress Catalog Card Number : 95-71880

———————————————————

ACKNOWLEDGMENTS

This work is a collaboration between the author and many providers of information. I am left owing a larger debt of gratitude to a longer list of contributors than I can ever repay or acknowledge properly. I pray the product is worthy of their efforts. My sincerest thanks to this partial list of participants:

Ron Arnold . . . Bellevue, Washington
Dr. Peter Strittmatter . . . Tucson, Arizona
Gene Ballinger . . . Hatch, New Mexico
Dena Clark . . . Morenci, Arizona
Andy Kurtz . . . Phoenix, Arizona
Jim Kennedy . . . Safford, Arizona
Margaret Gabbard . . . Boise, Idaho
Stanley Walters . . . Lakeview, Oregon
Chuck Cushman . . . Battle Ground, Washington
Donn Zea . . . Sacramento, California
Joe Carter . . . Safford, Arizona
Hank Ingram . . . Pittsburgh, Pennsylvania
Ken Evans . . . Yuma, Arizona
Tom Kelly . . . Deming, New Mexico
George Gordon . . . Isabella, Missouri
Ed Geiersbach . . . Oak Grove, Missouri
Debbie Daniels . . . Tucson, Arizona
Penny Hancock . . . Sacramento, California
Linda Deen . . . Kearny, Arizona

* * *

I pledge allegiance to the flag
of the United States of America,
and to the Republic for which it stands,
one nation under God, indivisible,
with liberty and justice for all.

Dedication:

For the children . . .
—April 19, 1993
—April 19, 1995

✝

In memory of Gil Murray

* * *

CONTENTS

Fighting Back

FOREWORD

The free citizens of the United States of America are facing ever-increasing threats to life, liberty and the pursuit of happiness. Bureaucrats ignore our constitutionally guaranteed unalienable rights. Environmental extremists embrace socialism. An arrogant federal government has outgrown the established pecking order of republican politics. Understanding the nature of government and the weaknesses of mankind, the Founding Fathers installed a feature in the Bill of Rights designed to head off the likelihood of these developments. It's called the Tenth Amendment. In the evolution of 20th century government it's been overlooked and forgotten, but that's changing.

Almost everywhere you go in political circles today, people and politicians are talking about the Tenth Amendment Movement. Governors are beginning to realize that if this movement is successful, they will be much more powerful than before. Those who do not fear this power— such as Governors Pete Wilson of California and Fife Symington of Arizona—are joining the rest of us in reclaiming state sovereignty. In time, most governors should realize that standing in front of this train will only get them run over.

The enormous power afforded by the Tenth Amendment (when coupled with the Ninth) is indeed a little scary. Do we have the strong moral fiber to use those powers in ways beneficial to mankind? Are there statesmen and stateswomen out there who can engage in meaningful and detached dialogue about the true meaning of our Constitution and do it in ways designed to strengthen and nurture the sanctity of the individual?

Or shall we be consumed by our own self-interest? Will the entrenched forces that would subjugate freedom be successful in preserving their own power? Has a firmly established oppressive force ever willingly and peacefully surrendered its power and elevated the opposed to equal status? There are many questions and few answers.

It is offered without proof that any reasonable solution to the nation's future direction will by definition have active participation by the people. Thomas Jefferson correctly believed that an educated people were not subject to rule by tyranny. In this age of information overload, sifting the gold nuggets of wisdom from all the intellectual trash will require both learning and debate by the people— not just those in power. The good news is: if the people do participate, we can almost certainly save our nation by peaceful, constitutional means.

The Tenth Amendment reads: "*The powers not delegated to the United States by the Constitution, nor prohibited by it to the States, are reserved to the States, respectively, or to the people.*" There are two basic, almost axiomatic, meanings to the Tenth.

First, the Federal Government has only those powers explicitly granted to it by the Constitution. By design of the Framers, it has no power that is not expressly spelled out.

The second meaning is: the States have any power they choose, whether expressly identified or not, so long as the Constitution does not prohibit it. This second meaning is what grants such awesome power to the States—any conceivable power *not prohibited* by the Constitution!

As if to emphasize our freedom, the Framers included the Ninth Amendment: "*The enumeration in the Constitution, of certain rights, shall not be construed to deny or disparage others retained by the people.*" In other words, just because certain rights are enumerated by the Constitution, we are not limited to those. There may be others we recognize. The Tenth Amendment leaves the exact definition and nature of these rights to the States, and they may vary from state to state.

It is essential that many people participate in the debate of these and other important ideas. There is no idea too large or too small. No one's opinion should be left out or considered unimportant. Remember, the Framers of our great Constitution understood accurately the nature of oppressive government. The challenge today is for us to accurately understand the nature of events in 1776 that established our freedom.

The Endangered American Dream is one of those aforementioned "gold nuggets of wisdom." In his book *Surviving the Second Civil War*, Timothy Robert Walters identified property as a fundamental tenet of human liberty. Later, this son of an Oregon farmer co-wrote *Government, GOD and Freedom* with Arizona Sheriff Richard Mack, in which he again heralded the "sanctity of property" as equal to life and liberty. The Founding Fathers saw it that way, too, just as they recognized that federal government should be subservient to the States. Without property, freedom becomes serfdom. Without state sovereignty, government is tyranny. The Tenth Amendment Movement was born of these truths. Walters uses *The Endangered American Dream* to show how clearly he understands the nature of oppressive government. He tells the truth and documents the incredible. And, importantly, he offers a variety of ways for informed Americans to participate in the debate.

I am proud to share this path toward reclaiming the American Republic. We should all embrace and celebrate the message.

Charles R. Duke
Colorado Senator, District 9

Charles R. Duke was elected to the Colorado Legislature in 1988, and served four years as a state representative before being elected to the Senate in 1994. As principle author of the Tenth Amendment Resolution in 1994, he has gained national attention in his efforts to garner support from the several states. When he is not on the road with his message, he writes a political column and works as an associate professor at the Colorado Technical University in Colorado Springs. The story of the Tenth Amendment Movement begins on page 184.

INTRODUCTION

The single most important thread of argument that runs through the several chapters and many issues addressed in this book is: *property is sacred!* To own property is a God-given right. Throughout history the ownership of property has translated to the most fundamental civil liberties. The Founding Fathers of our birthing nation recognized this, having fresh in their mouths the bitter taste of feudalism from the countries of Western Europe.

The Founding Fathers drew upon their knowledge of history, the observations of the great philosophers, their religious convictions and the concept of natural law to formulate the basis for the most unique and successful experiment in national government ever to occur—the American Republic. The entire recipe was comprised of three basic ingredients—three fundamental articles of freedom. They were: (1) the right to personal security (life); (2) the right to personal liberty (freedom); and (3) the right to own and work private property (the pursuit of happiness).

Not one of these articles was considered more important than another. They were intertwined and dependent upon one another. The framers of the U.S. Constitution and its Bill of Rights understood that to own private property was to possess freedom, to be secure in one's personal life and pursuit of happiness. To own and manage a piece of private property was to rise above the conditions of servitude, serfdom and slavery, and to no longer fear reprehension by abusive landlords and other officials representing an oppressive government.

John Adams, sometime between signing the Declaration of Independence and becoming the nation's second president, said, "The moment the idea is admitted into society that property is not as sacred as the laws of God . . . [then] anarchy and tyranny commence. Property must be secured or liberty cannot exist."

. . . as sacred as the laws of God . . .
Property must be secured or liberty cannot exist.

We have drifted far from that concept of private property. As government has grown during the last half of the 20th century, so has its compulsion to regulate. Regulation equates to control. Hundreds of laws have been enacted containing thousands of obscure clauses that infringe on the concept of Creator-endowed property rights. The Constitution does not *grant* property rights; it only promises to *protect* them. Regulatory agencies of the Federal Government have long demonstrated that property is no longer secure under constitutional guarantee. Millions of Americans have come to believe one of their most basic civil liberties is in jeopardy. Others have seen their rights to private property stripped away entirely by bureaucratic regulation. Some of their stories are told within the pages of this book.

The abuses do not come from any single source. Well-intended pieces of legislation such as the Endangered Species Act and Clean Water Act, both enacted during the 1970s, have been interpreted and applied in ways never imagined by the lawmakers who passed them. Preservationist groups commonly file lawsuits before sympathetic judges to lock down property. A well-organized environmental lobby has convinced urban legislators (and mainstream media) that "property rights" means "pollution rights." Enormous bureaucracies have been built under the umbrellas of cabinet-level departments—Interior, Agriculture, Housing and Urban Development, etc.—and every bureaucracy is under mandate to regulate (control) something. The Environmental Protection Agency (an independent agency under nobody's umbrella) is busy setting policy on property and regulating, fining, prosecuting and punishing property owners at will.

Many landowners across America felt a wave of hope for the future when their popular vote changed the face of Congress on November 8, 1994. For the first time in over 40 years control of both the House and Senate was in conservative Republican hands. Disappointingly, however, the new Congress does not have the physical or procedural means to change or fix all the bad laws, redefine the interpretations, lift the thousands of regulations, undo the damage and right all the wrongs. Therefore, while some areas of over-regulation may be examined and adjusted, others will remain virtually unchanged. The fight for individual property rights will continue to be fought on a case-specific basis.

These are the kinds of stories contained within this book. Environmentalists and bureaucrats alike have claimed—even before a 1995 congressional task force on private property rights—that there are no documentable incidents of government regulations resulting in the "taking" of private property. This book provides the documentation and shoots that assertion full of holes.

Regulatory agencies are going to continue to regulate. Radical preservationists are going to file even more lawsuits as Congress modifies environmental laws. Appellate and Supreme Court panels will continue to legislate by way of interpretation. Bureaucrats fearing for their jobs—and even some bureaucracies fearing for their lives under the congressional ax—will attempt to prove their value by becoming even more tenacious in their respective missions.

Abuses against private property rights will never stop entirely. However, they can be greatly diminished. Property rights advocates must go on the offensive—just as their opponents have been for many years. The same strategies are available to both sides. Coalitions of advocacy groups, including farmers, developers, realtors and local governments, make loud noises when lobbying on Capitol Hill. Lawsuits are effective weapons *against* bureaucracies and bureaucrats, environmental groups and their individual activists. There are several legal foundations and their attorneys who will take on these cases at little or no cost to the plaintiffs. This book provides some of that information.

Truth is truth, and right is right. No government has ever been successful, no nation has ever prospered, that did not recognize the God-given right of its people to own and manage private property. In this book I want to emphasize the importance of property in the spectrum of civil liberties, in the application of free enterprise, in the structure of successful republican government and in the preservation of personal security and freedom.

No other tenet of republican government has done as much to ensure the domestic tranquility and promote the general welfare of the people of the United States of America—not the right to keep and bear arms, not the right of free speech, freedom of religion or any other. Arizona's Governor Fife Symington wrote in 1994: "Consider the greatness of this nation and its historical gift for generating capital and wealth. There has never been anything like it in the history of mankind. And from the beginning, these things have been built entirely on a foundation of private property rights. That's where it begins and that's where it ends. That's the cradle of freedom."

It's my desire that this book will provide a candle of hope along the path of unalienable rights, as charted by our Creator and dedicated by the Founding Fathers of this nation. God bless those who work to preserve our American "cradle of freedom."

Timothy Robert Walters

American Dreams

and

Bureaucratic

Reality

A Nice Sanctuary

"The right to hold property is a natural right. It is the safeguard of family life, the stimulus and reward of work."
—Pastoral Letter of the
French Roman Catholic Hierarchy, 1919

When Robert Brace bought his father's homestead farm in 1975, he had no idea he was buying a nightmare. The acreage near Waterford, Pennsylvania, had been a beef and dairy farm, but Brace thought he would work it into his truck farm operation. Thirty years a vegetable farmer, Brace believed he could convert the pastures and some existing cropland to suit his needs.

Robert Brace Farms, Inc., worked the newly-acquired farm for more than a decade. Bob Brace and his sons, Ronnie and Randy, maintained a ten-year conservation project on the land, which included regular cleaning of an existing system of drainage ditches. In 1987 a colony of beavers moved in and built a dam in one of the ditches, blocking the natural flow of water and interfering with normal farming practices.

Brace reported the problem. In May of that year, two wildlife specialists arrived from the Pennsylvania Game Commission (PGC) to take the beavers out of the drainage system. One of those individuals was a man named Andrew Martin.

The Brace farm, by this time, was in excellent condition. The years of planning and thoughtful management had transformed the property into a picturebook setting. Andrew Martin looked around and said he thought the farm would "make a nice sanctuary." He asked Bob Brace to show his permits for cleaning the ditches. He was not impressed or convinced by Brace's explanation that regular cleaning of the ditches was allowed under agricultural exemptions.

Bob Brace and Andrew Martin were not stepping to the same fiddler. A verbal exchange resulted between them and ended abruptly when Martin told Brace "he didn't know what trouble could be." Within a few days the Brace farm was crawling with uninvited federal, state and local officials excavating soil and identifying plant species.

Two months later the Brace family received notice from four different federal and state regulatory agencies that they were in violation of "wetlands" provisions in the Clean Water Act. The Environmental Protection Agency (EPA), the Corps of Engineers (COE), the U.S. Fish and Wildlife Service (FWS) and the Pennsylvania Department of Environmental Resources (DER) had determined that the Braces were guilty of filling wetlands while cleaning their drainage ditches. They were ordered to "restore" the property to its original condition or face penalties exceeding $100,000 per day and possible imprisonment.

Bob Brace decided to stand his ground, literally. The case went to federal district court. Brace won, but not until *seven years later!* District Judge Glenn Mercer exonerated Robert Brace and Robert Brace Farms, Inc., of all charges aimed at him from the U.S. Department of Justice. Mercer, upon visiting the Brace farm, noted that less than a fourth of the land at issue even met the definition of a wetland. He found in his judgment for Brace:

> *This certainly does not appear to be the type of case where a corporation or large farming enterprise takes control of a parcel of land and dramatically alters the composition of the land and runs roughshod over the requirements of the Clean Water Act.*

The regulatory agencies hate to lose control of any portion of what they decide is *theirs*. Therefore, Bob Brace found his reprieve short-lived. Sixty days after Judge Mercer's ruling (the last day possible), the Department of Justice filed a notice of appeal. Brace said reflectively, "It's changed the way I look at everything. Land use regulations have become so over-burdensome and confiscatory that there's no longer any incentive for property owners and businesses to continue risking everything day after day."

Unfortunately, that's exactly how the control-greedy powercrats of the regulatory government bureaucracies want Bob Brace and other landowners to feel. It makes their jobs easier. Regulation equates to control. To control a man's property is to control the man. Big government and its offspring bureaucracies are self-conditioned to thrive on control. The freedom of a property owner to manage and work his own land without government intervention (as intended by the Founding Fathers) is the highest obstacle in the path of total government control. Alas, the sword of control has many sharp edges.

The Third U.S. Circuit Court of Appeals in Philadelphia *reversed* Judge Mercer's ruling. The appellate court found instead that Robert Brace was *not* entitled to agricultural exemption in his cleaning of the drainage ditches and, therefore, had violated Section 404 of the Clean Water Act by not filing for a permit. The conservation benefits derived from maintaining the drainage system for ten years *before* the land was declared a wetland did not matter to the court. Nor did it matter that there was no reason to get a permit—and no law to break by *not* getting a permit—until *after* the run-in with Andrew Martin resulted in the cursory designation of the property as a wetland. The order to "restore" the property was upheld and the case turned back to the district court for handling of the restoration order and deciding civil penalties. Robert Brace requested a review of his case before the U.S. Supreme Court.

Bob Brace's attorney Henry Ingram said, "The odds are about 4,000-to-one that the court will accept the request." He added, "Bob Brace is now subject to millions of dollars in civil penalties because he's been 'in violation' for a long time." Ingram says Robert Brace is a "man of great strength and character," but more than eight years of bureaucratic persecution over what Brace believed was conscientious management practices on his own land have taken a heavy toll—physically and emotionally. In June, 1995, Ingram said Pennsylvania Governor Tom Ridge was beginning to lose interest in the long-running issue. A bank had canceled its line of credit to the Brace farm. Ingram emphasized, too, that "to comply with the restoration order will destroy the drainage system and ruin the farm."

Brace noted during the bureaucratic melee over his farm that "the government didn't have to prove that what I did harmed the environment or caused harm to my neighbors." An allegation of wrongdoing prompted by a vindictive bureaucrat is all it took to inflame four government agencies and the U.S. Department of Justice against one honest farmer.

Robert Brace summed it up. "Without private property ownership and a strong economy, everyone loses, including private citizens who depend upon the existence of the business community for *their* livelihoods. People need to realize that their voice *does* make a difference, and that the days of thinking things will magically get better or that 'someone else will take care of it' are over. They need to contact their congressmen and senators about the unfairness of it all . . . *before* it's too late."

On June 26, 1995, the Supreme Court—without explanation—refused to hear Brace's appeal. Short of congressional intervention, there is no higher level of authority. Faced with a court order to, in effect, convert his own farm into a wetland sanctuary, Brace reflected, "I've gotten to know the ways of the legal, legislative and judicial systems . . . They aren't much help to ordinary citizens like me."

Incidentally, Andrew Martin left the Pennsylvania Game Commission a short time after starting Bob Brace's nightmare. As a self-proclaimed "wetland and environmental specialist," he formed his own company, Andrew Martin & Associates. In a subsequent interview with the *Erie Times*, he boasted, "My business is driven by regulations."[1]

The Billboard at Port Bolivar

"Private property rights lie near the source of the liberty under which Americans are free to enjoy the God-given beauty of the Earth. It is the nature of government to constantly close in upon that liberty, to diminish it, to consume it."

—Fife Symington
Governor of Arizona, 1992

Marinus Van Leuzen is a crusty Dutchman who lives at Port Bolivar, Texas. His experience with the Corps of Engineers (COE) and a U.S. District Court represents the apex of bureaucratic zeal and judicial arrogance.

Van Leuzen narrowly escaped the Nazi invasion of Holland in 1939. He spent most of World War II working on supply convoys to Europe and Russia with the U.S. Merchant Marines. After the war he opened a tavern near Corpus Christi, followed by a service station in Galveston. Finally, he built the Last Stop Motel at Port Bolivar, a

---

1-This story was printed in part in the *Pennsylvania Landowner*, Vol. VII, No. 1, pp.1-2, April 1994. Additional information provided by Hank Ingram, Buchanan Ingersoll, P.C., 600 Grant Street, 57th Floor, Pittsburgh, PA 15219.

fishing village near the tip of Bolivar Peninsula overlooking the waters of Galveston Bay.

For 25 years prior to 1989, Van Leuzen had owned a small wedge of property adjacent to the motel. The half-acre parcel separated Highway 87 from the bay. It had previously been home to an unsightly bait shop next to a marina built and operated by Van Leuzen's son-in-law. At age 73, Van Leuzen decided to move his home to the available property so he would be near his business and family.

Van Leuzen obtained a building permit from Galveston County, then went to work. He hired a contractor to bring in fill dirt to clean and level the property and to begin erecting his home. The project was in full swing when Paula Wise arrived.

She came onto the property shouting, "Stop the work! Stop the work!"

The salty Dutchman recalls approaching the intruder and inquiring, "Who the hell are you?"

The woman identified herself as an agent with the COE.

Van Leuzen told her simply, "I don't give a damn who you are, get your ass off my property."

Paula Wise did as she was told, but not before assuring Van Leuzen that she was about to become a very big part of his life. She was not lying.

The Galveston Enforcement Division of the Corps of Engineers (Paula Wise's department) accused Van Leuzen of dumping truckloads of fill dirt on a federally protected wetland. The old Dutchman scoffed at the accusation because his land was several feet above sea level

—even at high tide—and was never wet with standing water. Further, he believed his property was legally classified as "upland," just as the COE had designated his son-in-law's adjoining parcel to accommodate a marina years earlier. Cease-and-desist orders came from the COE and the EPA. Van Leuzen ignored them and went on with his project. The old man would not be intimidated. Federal regulators apparently decided to make an example of him after he told an armed agent who came trespassing, "You're probably not old enough to pee over your boots."

The insult was too much for the bureaucrats to take from a stubborn old property owner. They launched a full-scale investigation. Like a scene from *Dick Tracy*, they began videotaping the activity on Van Leuzen's property from a nearby rooftop. Then they filed suit in federal court.

Ken McCasland, a close friend of Van Leuzen from Galveston, said, "They probably spent half a million on this case, with all the experts they kept flying in."

Finally, in March of 1993 (nearly *four years* after the alleged violations), the case was decided. U.S. District Judge Samuel Kent wrote a cumbersome 39-page decision, even drawing on some colorful embellishment from the science-fiction works of Kurt Vonnegut and Michael Crichton. He fined Van Leuzen's contractor $900, then turned his wrath to the old man's *"willful and brazen disregard for the rule of the law and the integrity of the environment."* Apparently swimming in the juice of creativity, Judge Kent referred to Van Leuzen as *"a classic example of why . . . our world is literally 'going to hell in a handbasket'."* He went on, *"Attitudes like Defendant Van*

Leuzen's are beyond selfishness. Unchecked, they are the seeds of national, environmental suicide."

Marinus Van Leuzen's so-called "selfishness" was his desire to put *his* house on a tiny piece of dry land which *he* owned and had paid taxes on for a quarter of a century. He did not know his land had been identified as a "wetland" and had no reason to believe it was any different from his son-in-law's adjacent "upland" parcel. How does leveling a spot for a house on a private lot become a seed of "national, environmental suicide?"

Judge Kent decided to make an example of Van Leuzen—just as COE officials wanted. The cranky old Dutchman (by now living in his house on the property) was ordered to remove about four dozen truckloads of fill from the site, then restore and revegetate the area. His septic tank and house also were to be moved. Kent further decreed that Van Leuzen's income would be garnished in the amount of $350 per month for up to *12 years* in order to establish an escrow fund for removal of the home.

Judge Kent then struck his most spiteful blow. Motorists passing Van Leuzen's property along Highway 87 slow down to gaze in wonder at the huge billboard standing in the old man's front yard. It reads:

WETLANDS RESTORATION

ILLEGAL FILL MATERIAL DEPOSITED WITHOUT REQUIRED PERMIT FROM THE U.S. ARMY CORPS OF ENGINEERS BY M. VAN LEUZEN IS BEING REMOVED BY THE FILLER AT HIS OWN EXPENSE. IN ADDITION, THE WETLANDS SHALL BE REVEGETATED AND CIVIL PENALTIES PAID. FINAL RESTORATION OF THE

PROPERTY, INCLUDING RELOCATION OF THE HOUSE, SHALL BE FUNDED BY M. VAN LEUZEN.

AS ORDERED BY THE U.S. DISTRICT COURT FOR THE SOUTHERN DISTRICT OF TEXAS, GALVESTON DIVISION, ON BEHALF OF THE U.S. ARMY CORPS OF ENGINEERS AND THE U.S. ENVIRONMENTAL PROTECTION AGENCY.

Ken McCasland said, "He barely escaped the Nazis and the Japanese, and then to wind up here with his own government doing this to him."

Carol LaGrasse, who heads Property Rights Foundation of America in New York, decries the behavior of COE agents, EPA officials and Judge Samuel Kent. "They used Marinus Van Leuzen as a pseudo-scapegoat for the environmental woes of the planet."

The old Dutchman who refused to be intimidated and never lost his sense of humor finds a generous portion of irony in the presence of a watery lowland now circling three sides of his house. He was ordered to restore a piece of dry land and the 50 truckloads of fill he was forced to haul away *created* a "wetland" where there never had been one before.[2]

Regulatory abuses, such as those suffered by Robert Brace and Marinus Van Leuzen, are not unique to any one part of the country. Documented horror stories of bureaucratic extremism and environmental overkill affecting

---

2-Various renderings of Marinus Van Leuzen's story have appeared in different publications and periodicals. Most details contained here were presented by John MacCormack, staff writer for *San Antonio Express-News*, Monday edition, September 26, 1994, pp. 1A & 4A.

property rights and land uses abound from Florida to Alaska, from Maine to Hawaii. They come in many different forms over a variety of regulations and issues.

Nancie G. Marzulla, chief legal counsel for Washington, DC-based Defenders of Property Rights, says, "Wetlands enforcement is just one of the many areas where government has trampled on people's constitutional rights to use their property in a reasonable manner." Marzulla adds that, in the truest definition, property is much more than just land—labor and services, personal possessions, ideas, consumer products, businesses, buildings and machines. She believes economic decisions and personal choices of millions of Americans are based largely on concerns for property. But most people are quickly intimidated by government agents referencing mountains of regulations, even when there was never any intent of wrongdoing. Common citizens have a natural tendency to perceive government "officials" as figures of authority and power. In most cases the regulatory abuses are applied by ambitious bureaucrats to private citizens who believed they were obeying the law at the time of their so-called "violations."

One such couple, Gaston and Monique Roberge of Old Orchard Beach, Maine, tried to sell less than three acres of property to a developer who had offered them $440,000. They had owned the parcel for over 25 years. The deal went sour when the Corps of Engineers told the developer the lot was a "wetland" under its legal jurisdiction. The elderly couple received an order from the COE, under wetlands provisions of the Clean Water Act, to remove thousands of square feet of dirt placed on their property a decade earlier by the city. The projected cost would be more than

$50,000. The *Washington Times* reported that an internal COE memo, written by one Jay Clement, declared: "Roberge would be a good one to squash and set an example."

Bureaucrats in the business of enforcing regulations love to make examples. The COE succeeded in doing so with Ronald Angelocci. The Michigan property owner hauled some dirt onto his lot to help eradicate the weeds responsible for inflaming his wife's allergies. His "violation" of the Clean Water Act landed him in jail. A New York couple were fined $30,000 for adding a deck to their home and causing a shadow to fall across a "wetland." John Poszgai of Morristown, Pennsylvania, spent nearly three years in federal prison before being released on condition that he "restore" his private creekbank with the old tires and car parts he'd removed while "disturbing a wetland."

Where is the common sense? Where's the intelligence? Before the 104th Congress invoked a temporary moratorium on new regulations in early 1995, federal regulatory agencies were adding more than 200 pages of new rules and unlegislated "statutes" to the *Federal Register* every day. The moratorium did not remove any of those rules already published. Once a rule is in place in the *Register*, it is embraced as law by the regulators. Rewriting the entire spectrum of inequitable provisions from many pieces of federal legislation would not cause most of these regulations to magically disappear. Without the regulations many government agencies would be without a purpose. Power-driven bureaucrats live by those regulations, depend on them for their livelihoods and defend them fiercely.

Robert Brace and Marinus Van Leuzen, John Poszgai, Gaston Roberge and thousands of other American property owners have made "economic decisions and personal choices" in the management and use of their properties. As a result they have been singled out, attacked, persecuted, prosecuted and sometimes destroyed by single-minded bureaucrats seeking to justify their jobs. More often than not the court system fails to find in favor of property owners because federal judges tend to align themselves with their employer—the Federal Government.

For these reasons the old Dutchman at Port Bolivar, Texas, must vacate his own property, remove all his possessions from it—*including his house!*—and let the land lay idle as an unnatural wetland. He will still be allowed to pay his taxes, however—the only claim to the parcel he has left. When Marinus Van Leuzen migrated from Holland more than 50 years ago he brought with him a far different understanding of the American Dream.

The Lost Pursuit

"The only dependable foundation of personal liberty is the personal economic security of private property."
—Walter A. Lippman
American journalist, 1934

A scary evolution-of-thought process has led to the attitude among eco-preservationists and many control-driven bureaucrats that government has absolute authority over the rights of property owners. It is the result of a few decades of growing momentum in efforts to protect and "manage" everything that walks, crawls, swims or flies, not to mention what grows or is extracted out of the ground. It comes from a burgeoning government dependent upon reams of new regulations each year that justify its costly growth and activities. It is fueled by Supreme Court interpretations that provide for the superiority of species and resources over humankind, no matter the impact. And, perhaps, it is the product of an unwary society that believes the civil rights and liberties enjoyed in this country are eternal, steadfast and invulnerable.

The Founding Fathers knew that to take freedom for granted was to lose it. That is why the Constitution was written to *protect* rights granted by God, and the Bill of Rights was installed to further protect the Constitution. The right to own and manage private property was given equal footing with the rights to life and liberty. Under the founding documents, government was forbidden from seizing, restricting the use of and decreasing the value of a freeman's property just as strictly as it was from seizing, restricting the use of and decreasing the value of a freeman's *life!* Only by recognizing property as *sacred* and the rights to it as "*Creator-endowed*" would the rights to life and other civil liberties remain secure.

Dr. Bruce Yandle, Alumni Professor of Economics and Legal Studies at Clemson University, believes even in today's society that property rights are part of "an ethical system which serves as a foundation for social order." Echoing the Founders' convictions, Yandle adds, "Property rights are not things created in Washington that can be manipulated to serve some expedient interest. To put it simply, we do not have property rights because of law. We have law because of property rights."

Ken Evans, President of the Arizona Farm Bureau Federation, thinks government has somehow gotten it backwards. Testifying before a congressional task force on property rights in June of 1995, Evans said, " . . . the framers of the Constitution envisioned a government where the rights of individuals to own and responsibly use property to pursue their dreams was inalienable, and the proper role of government was limited to . . . protection of those enumerated *personal* rights to life, liberty and the pursuit of happiness. Somewhere in our 200- year journey we took a left turn."

Among the casualties of the "left turn" is a California man who owns a parcel of coastal property, part upland and part potential wetland. He wanted to develop the property and applied for a permit to fill the "wetland," although the area had never been officially designated as such. In response to the permit application the U.S. Fish and Wildlife Service (FWS) surveyed the property. Agents informed the owner that his lowland property was inhabited by the salt marsh harvest mouse, a rodent subspecies protected by the Endangered Species Act. The federal agency quickly designated the lower-elevation property a "critical habitat." No development would be allowed there because it might disturb the harvest mouse. Further, the upland property was declared "undevelopable." Why? FWS officials explained that a possible trend in global warming might cause the polar ice caps to melt. In that event the lower "wetland" could become inundated, forcing the endangered mice to relocate on the upland property.[3]

The regulatory bureaucracies have acquired a dangerous amount of power. They have swelled up with self-authorized importance until they feel they do not have to account to anyone but themselves—and for the most part, they are right. Commonly, administrative appointees are given nearly unlimited authority to make decisions, set policy and enforce regulations with the same effects as legislated statutes. Agents in regional offices operate almost unchecked. For example, the Secretary of the Interior (charged with overseeing the Bureau of Land Management, the National Park Service, the Bureau of Reclamation, the U.S. Fish and Wildlife Service and more) cannot possibly supervise all his tens of thousands of staff spread out across the 50 states. Every agent in every capacity holds some position of "authority." They make decisions and enforce regulations as they interpret them. Excepting only some rare and isolated instances, they enjoy the blessings of their Washington leadership. And the courts tend to prop up the legitimacy of the large bureaucracies.

The agencies justify their behavior by pointing out the need to protect endangered species, to manage wetlands

---

3-A story paraphrased in conservative publications, including the *San Diego Union-Tribune*, by columnist Joseph Perkins, but largely avoided by conservation advocates because it is so "undefendable." An account of documentation appears in *Grand Theft and Petit Larceny: Property Rights in America*, Mark L. Pollot, Pacific Research Institute for Public Policy, San Francisco, CA, 1993, p. 159.

and critical habitat, to preserve rivers and lakes and other natural wonders. But few of them (or their agents) can draw a discernible line between managing their interests and controlling *people*. Most of them believe that to manage or protect a species or resource they *must* control the people around it. Any disciplinarian will agree it's easier to achieve *total* control over a subject than it is to maintain *partial* control and allow some privileges.

The partial control of property in California inhabited by the salt marsh harvest mouse would have created unwanted management problems for the FWS. Therefore, total control was the preferred option. The landowner's God-given, constitutionally guaranteed property rights were not considered—only the agency's need for control—and the owner was restricted from doing *anything* with his property.

John and Josephine Bronczyk of Anoka County, Minnesota, know about total control. Nine acres at the southern edge of the Bronczyks' property are covered by a lake. They know it's a wetland. John Bronczyk says, "There's nobody who's got more respect for wetlands than we do." The state declared the area a "public waters wetland," meaning it was off-limits to any development by its owners, but it was open to the public for hunting and other recreation. The elderly Bronczyk siblings then learned that an additional 104 acres of solid land were included in the designation, leaving only 47 acres of their 160-acre farm unrestricted. John Bronczyk believes, "It's worth something when you can call it your own. But when the public can come on it, it's worthless."

The Bronczyks sued, asking that only the nine acres of marshland be designated a wetland or the state pay "just compensation" for their loss.

Kent Lokkesmoe, an official with the state's Department of Natural Resources, calls the Bronczyk lawsuit "frivolous."

Bronczyk says, "We feel a person's property rights are sacred."[4]

Property rights are sacred!

Again, the Founding Fathers' deepest convictions manifested themselves in the importance of private property. Freedom cannot survive without private property. Free enterprise will collapse without the right to manage and use private property. Free republican government will not stand up against the encroaching forces of socialism without the preservation of private property rights.

"Takings" became the battle cry under the new Congress of 1995. Landowners across the nation started getting the attention of lawmakers on both sides of the issue. They sought protection from government confiscation of their property and "just compensation" if use of their land became restricted or its value decreased by regulatory intervention. They gained credibility by documenting hundreds of stories of property rights abuses at the hands of government officials. The Fifth Amendment became their sword and war shield:

4-Details included in a story by Carolyn Pesce, *USA Today*, Monday edition, February 6, 1995, p. 3A.

> *No person shall be . . . deprived of life, liberty, or property, without due process of law; nor shall private property be taken for public use without just compensation.*

Richard Epstein, author of *Takings* (a book that closely examines the Constitution and Fifth Amendment), says a prime danger exists in the public tendency "to get so upset about government that you think private ownership means unlimited use of land." While extremes will occur in any movement, responsible property owners are not asking for "unlimited" use of their land. They know that with land ownership comes responsibility. Most land owners are excellent stewards because along with land ownership and responsibility comes a thing called pride. Many laws exist in every state to guard against the offenses of the prideless few who cause nuisance, pollute and threaten their neighbors' rights or the welfare of the general public.

Environmentalists claim property owners are using their so-called "rights" to justify gutting important environmental laws that get in their way. Even Vice President Al Gore sharply criticized attempts in the 104th Congress to force government agencies to take a more cautious approach toward taking private property. Again, the whole debate comes back to the issue of control— complete or partial.

Ken Evans (Arizona Farm Bureau) says, "The rights of individuals to own and use private property predate the existence of governments. This is often called 'natural law' or natural rights. Our Declaration of Independence states ' . . . *that they are endowed by their Creator with certain unalienable Rights* . . . ' Governments are then created to protect the rights that individuals already possess. The Declaration of Independence continues, '*That to secure these rights, Governments are instituted among Men, deriving their just powers from the consent of the governed* . . . ' That basic framework was carried over to the U.S. Constitution. To it was added the fifth amendment phrase, '. . . *nor shall private property be taken for public use, without just compensation.*' The writers of the Constitution and the Bill of Rights knew that governments would need to take property for legitimate reasons, and that just compensation was part of the eminent domain process. There was nothing new about the idea."

There's nothing new about it now—except that it's not being done. The Fifth Amendment protection of private property has been ignored—even treated as nonexistent—for decades by the Federal Government (and many state agencies as well). Property owners know, too, that governments will need to take property for legitimate reasons. They just want to be compensated for it.

What they *don't* want is to be suddenly informed that their back pasture is a beaver refuge or public park without remuneration for their loss. What they *do* want is the reassurance of believing their constitutional rights are still in place and that the American Dream has not been undermined by the loss of one its most important tenets of liberty.

Of Truth and Stratagem

"Private property rights are the soil in which our concept
of human rights grows and matures."
—Charles E. Whittaker
U.S. Supreme Court Justice, 1966

The Federal Government "owns" almost 40 percent
of the land area within the borders of the United States.
That includes Bureau of Land Management holdings in the
West, U.S. National Forests across the country, national
parks and monuments, military installations and testing
grounds, national rivers and conservation areas, wilderness
areas, wildlife refuges, historic sites and more. While most
of these areas are called "public lands," some intense efforts
are underway to remove all "public" activity from them.

Some examples? In May 1995, the U.S. Fish and
Wildlife Service designated nearly five million acres of
critical habitat for the Mexican spotted owl in Arizona,
Utah, Colorado and New Mexico, severely restricting all
previous uses of the land. The 1993 designation of nearly
2,000 miles of Colorado River and its tributaries in six
western states as critical habitat for four species of fish has
prevented hundreds of landowners from maintaining water
diversions and guarding against erosion. In January of 1995,
over 28 million acres of national forest land in Idaho (more
than half the state) were placed off-limits to managed

multiple-use activities in deference to an endangered salmon. The Desert Protection Act of 1994 "locked up" 6,600,000 acres of public land in southern California (approximately one-fourth of the state). The state of Texas sued the federal government over efforts to designate more than 20 million acres of public *and private* land in 33 counties as protected habitat for the golden-cheeked warbler. The Northern Rockies Ecosystem Protection Act of 1994 attempted to consign 13 million acres in five states to "wilderness" protection.

It's all about control. Some lawmakers are lending their interest to an environmentalist plan called the North American Wilderness Recovery Project, which would close roads, reclaim farms and communities, dismantle dams and powerlines and generally displace humans from about half of the nation. Ideally, then, the "wilderness" would be allowed to "rewild" itself.[5]

Further, the federal agencies are not satisfied managing and regulating what they have. They want more. Through the efforts of The Nature Conservancy (a private environmental organization) and other land acquisition channels, the Federal Government is busy acquiring *private property* from its citizens at an average rate of about 1,000 acres *per day!*[6]

5-The entire plan, its creators and supporters are discussed in *Surviving the Second Civil War: The Land Rights Battle . . . and How To Win It*, Timothy Robert Walters, Rawhide Western Publishing, Safford, AZ, 1994, pp. 136-140.

6-Detailed accounts in *Surviving the Second Civil War*, pp. 126-128.

The battle for control is a tenacious one. On one side of the debate are property owners, public lands users and those within the legislative bodies who still believe the Constitution is a live, working document and that citizens' fundamental civil rights should be protected by it. The opposite camp is driven by liberal, visionary politicians, parasitic bureaucrats who thrive on the adrenaline of power and eco-socialistic environmental preservationists.

Rhetoric and propaganda flow profusely in the war for control of the land. It's often hard to distinguish between facts and cleverly crafted lies.

There were many legislative attempts to preserve private property protection before the birth of the 104th Congress in 1995. The last one was a bill introduced by Texas Senator Phil Gramm in August of 1994. Gramm said the Private Property Rights Restoration Act would "restore the constitutional mandate that just compensation be paid when government action reduces private property value." The bill specified that when federal regulatory action caused the market value of a landowner's property to decrease by 25 percent or $10,000, then the property owner could sue for compensation. A successful claimant could either accept payment for the the devaluation and keep the property or deed the whole property to the government in exchange for payment at full market value.

Opponents of the bill said it would cause "an avalanche of lawsuits" and that it would "bust the budget" of the Federal Government. Nothing could have been further from the truth. The funds used to pay for actual "takings," as specified within the bill, would have come from the budgets of the agencies responsible for imposing

41

the regulations. And the law would serve to make bureaucrats more cautious than capricious.

There was never an illusion in anyone's mind that the bill would pass. But with a new Republican face on Congress in 1995, the chances for such a law became brighter. The promise of private property rights protection was an important clause in the Contract with America that helped install a Republican majority in the U.S. House of Representatives for the first time in nearly half a century.

On March 3, 1995, the House passed its own Private Property Rights Protection Act on a vote of 277 to 148. A major stipulation of the bill was compensation to a landowner whose property value is decreased by 20 percent due to environmental regulation.

Yelps of protest emanated from the preservationist community—as well as a concerted drive to confuse and mislead the American public. The Wilderness Society—an ultra-socialist organization long in bed with the U.S. Interior Department—generated a nationwide propaganda campaign. A multi-page mailing, soliciting return comments to former BLM Director Jim Baca, claimed, "Advocates of 'private property takings' bills say big-money interests should be free to do whatever they want on their land regardless of the consequences to others. If they are not allowed to do so, they must be paid off. It's a no-win choice for American homeowners and taxpayers."

The use of terms like "big money interests" is intended to anger common workaday citizens. Reference to "a no-win choice for American homeowners" is a stratagem to alienate property owners from the very legislation passed to protect them.

The Wilderness Society diatribe continues, "American taxpayers would be forced to pay a mining company . . . not to build its copper smelter next to a school, or a pornography king not to build his porno shop next to a day care center. If taxpayers can't afford the hefty price tag, takings laws say these landowners can build even if our children's health and safety are threatened. Takings proponents say . . . citizens whose health or property is damaged can always go to court *after* the damage is done."

There is not one shred of truth in that paragraph. It does, however, represent a common ploy—feigning concern for the welfare of children—to garner unwarranted support. Scare tactics are used frequently by those advocating (and thirsting for) control.

U.S. Congressman John Shadegg, Chairman of the 1995 Congressional Task Force on Private Property Rights, points up the fallacy. "It has been settled common law for many hundreds of years that people cannot use their property in ways that harm or threaten others. [And] Congress has passed other laws that . . . protect the public's safety, stopping nuisances or uses of property which are obnoxious or offensive to neighboring property owners."

The Private Property Rights Protection Act was aimed at *reducing* lawsuits, not creating more. Congressman Shadegg says, "American citizens should not have to sue the Federal Government to force it to respect their constitutional rights."

The Wilderness Society says, "The only way to prevent big-money interests from dumping toxins into a community's drinking water . . . is to pay them off."

Another lie. Pollution laws are still (and will

continue to be) very reliable safeguards against health and safety violations that threaten the public welfare. Farmers and ranchers alone (the agriculture industry) are monitored by an army of 130,000 federal regulators watching everything from pesticide applications to water consumption to ditch digging. John Hosemann, Chief Economist for the American Farm Bureau Federation, says the cost to private operators is close to 20 billion dollars a year. But as long as a regulation (or regulator) does not decrease the value of their property, then there is no "taking."

The Wilderness Society does not care about "American homeowners and taxpayers." Ron Arnold, Executive Vice President of the Center for the Defense of Free Enterprise, says, "The Wilderness Society really operates only a two-pronged strategy: to nationalize all private land possible, and to eliminate all free market use on government lands."[7] That means turning all private property over to the government, then not allowing anyone to make a living from it. In 1992, under the direction of its president George Frampton, the Society prepared a 292-page report on how to dismantle property rights on a state-by-state basis. (Frampton was later appointed Assistant Director of the Interior Department under Secretary Bruce Babbitt.)

Neither is the Society a stranger to "big-money interests." While espousing eco-socialistic politics, the (501)(c)(3) organization boasts an annual budget of

---

7-From *Trashing the Economy: How Runaway Environmentalism is Wrecking America*, Ron Arnold and Alan Gottlieb, Free Enterprise Press, Bellevue, WA, 1993, p. 305.

approximately 20 million dollars. More than ten percent of that is raised through grants from corporations and foundations like Archer Daniels Midland, Discount Corporation of America, Andrew W. Mellon Foundation, Morgan Guaranty Trust Company of New York, New York Times Foundation, Timberland Company, United Conveyor Corporation and many more.[8] On the list are corporations tied in various ways to mining, timber harvest, oil, manufacturing, farming and ranching.

The Wilderness Society is only a single example of dozens of anti-private property, anti-industry, anti-free enterprise, anti-capitalist, anti-American organizations in this country committed to destroying the foundations, customs and cultures and the convictions that made it great.

So whose rights to private property should be protected first? Eco-socialist environmentalists? Radical preservationists? Federal bureaucrats? Animal species? Or property owners?

Our Founding Fathers would have rallied around the landowners, as they did with raised muskets to free themselves from the oppression of their first general government and the tyranny of King George III. Two hundred years of self-government, however, seem to have attenuated the importance of private property.

Bruce Babbitt, former Governor of Arizona and Secretary of the Interior under President Clinton, expressed

---

8-Complete and partial profiles of several dozen environmental groups appear in *Trashing the Economy* (footnote 7). The complete profile on the Wilderness Society begins p. 299. Footnote 8, pp. 310-311.

a desire to change "the individualistic view of property," meaning one person should not be allowed to own any parcel unto himself. He advocated a more "communitarian interpretation" and emphasized, "You can't build fences around property."

Dave Foreman, founder of the eco-extremist group Earth First!, declared, "Our goal is to create a new political reality based on the needs of *other species*." (emphasis added).

Author Richard Stapleton wrote in the September/ October 1993 issue of *National Parks* magazine, "Ownership . . . is temporal. The land belongs to none of us." He added, " . . . it is a fight . . . against the belief that property is one of those inalienable rights endowed to us by our Creator through the Declaration of Independence."

Joni Bosh, former Chair of the Arizona Community Protection Committee, told Congressman Shadegg's property rights task force, "The horror stories that we have been hearing nationally just aren't as horrible as the proponents [of property rights] would like us to believe."

These people have forgotten the agony and sacrifice of the Founding Fathers forging a new free nation. They no longer recognize that the basic liberties of personal security, freedom and property are all tied together because separately they cannot endure. Without property, freedom becomes serfdom and personal security (life) is meaningless.

Mr. Babbitt has drawn his "communitarian" philosophies from the manifestoes of failed communist governments around the world. Dave Foreman scoffs at the meaning of Genesis 1:26.[9] Obviously, Richard Stapleton accepts only those parts of the U.S. Constitution that appeal to him or serve *his* agenda. And Joni Bosh should talk to Robert Brace or Marinus Van Leuzen about the severity and authenticity of their horror stories.

Those who undermine the significance of God-given property rights in deference to "communitarian" or socialistic philosophies have the right to do so because the U.S. Constitution guarantees their right of free speech. They would be outraged if federal regulators attempted to take that right away or diminish its effectiveness. The same fierce defense must be thrown up for *all* the tenets of liberty or none of them is secure. President John Adams left no doubt about the importance of private property: "The moment the idea is admitted into society that property is not as sacred as the laws of God . . . [then] anarchy and tyranny commence. Property must be secured or liberty cannot exist."

Anarchy and tyranny have commenced. An undercurrent of anger and suspicion toward government and its regulating agencies swirls across the heartland of America. The spread of these cancers will not abate so long as a single American citizen is " . . . *deprived of life, liberty, or **property**, without due process of law . . .* " (emphasis added).

9-*And God said, Let us make man in our image, after our likeness: and let them have dominion over the fish of the sea, and over the fowl of the air, and every other living thing that moveth upon the earth.* (Holy Bible, King James Version)

Land Lock

"The theory of the Communists may be summed up in a single sentence: Abolition of private property."
— Karl Marx and Fredrich Engels
"The Communist Manifesto," 1848

Russell Jacobs rues the day he acquired his "calcareous fen." In 1990, the Raymond, Wisconsin, postal worker bought a suburban plot of land with plans to build a home for his family there. Racine County officials assured Jacobs there would be no problem building his house on the parcel.

Jacobs' problems, however, did not lie with county government. It was the U.S. Army Corps of Engineers that informed the father of three that he would need a permit from the COE to build *his* dream home on *their* designated "calcareous fen"—a limestone-supported piece of ground not quite wet enough to be considered a marsh, but still somehow included in the loose definition of a "wetland."

Jacobs applied for the required permit. The COE responded by mail—*242 days later!*—that his application was denied. The COE's Richard W. Craig wrote summarily, "I have determined that issuance of the requested permit would be contrary to the public interest." Craig's cursory decision effectively separated Jacobs from his property, his dream of building a home on it and his constitutional protection of life, liberty and the pursuit of happiness.[10]

Contrary to the public interest?

What possible "public interest" could be vested in Russell Jacobs' half-acre suburban plot? The COE never defined its ecological significance. Richard Craig never explained his "concern." The property was not the site of hiking trails, campsites, fishing holes or bird-watching blinds. No archaeological ruins existed there. No endangered animals or fish resided there. The land was not critical to supporting sensitive flora. It was a tiny plot of ground that no one noticed, needed or cared about—except the family who shouldered the financial and tax responsibility for it and planned to live on it.

There was no "public interest" in the property!

There was *bureaucratic* interest, however, because the whole issue of property rights is about *who controls the land.* "Public interest" is a catch phrase used by federal agencies and environmental groups to justify almost any kind of infringement on the rights and legal activities of property owners and public lands users.

The obvious example, of course, is the justified (and accepted) acquisition of rights-of-way for the construction of a highway. In this application the land is paid for and transferred to its new owner for inclusion in the project. Landowners who refuse to sell usually face condemnation proceedings as a part of the eminent domain process, and

_____

10-*Wall Street Journal*, "Property Rights and Wrongs," Jonathan
 Tolman, Tuesday edition, January 17, 1995, editorial page. Tolman
 is an analyst at the Competitive Enterprise Institute, Washington, DC.

they ultimately lose the property anyway. Pursuant to the Fifth Amendment to the Constitution, however, they are still paid for their losses.

On the other hand, there is a myriad of examples that do not fall under the eminent domain process. Robert Brace, under court order to turn his farm into a wetland, has lost the use and value of his property through federal regulatory action and he will not be compensated. Marinus Van Leuzen, forced to move his house off his own land under wetlands protection enforcement, will not be compensated. Hundreds of farmers cannot protect their riverside properties from erosion due to "critical habitat" designations for endangered species of fish in the streams. Their land washes away and the value of remaining portions plummets. Thousands of private landowners find themselves restricted from harvesting resources, such as trees and minerals, by government claims of endangered species protection. Their livelihoods suffer and there is no hope for remuneration.

When the U.S. Fish and Wildlife Service determines that a two-and-one-half-mile radius must be protected around every nesting pair of northern spotted owls, then "refuges" for the birds have been established. Government officials and eco-preservationists argue that it's in the "public interest" to protect the birds. Similarly, prohibiting riverside landowners from protecting or repairing their streambank properties also sets up designated "refuges" for wildlife. It's in the "public interest" to protect the fish. The regulating bureaucracies of the Federal Government know they cannot possibly pay for all the land they are locking up from the landowners so they refrain from making their "wildlife refuges" a part of the National Wildlife Refuge system. They do not name them or ask for congressional approval. The result is the same. Government agencies control the land and landowners are "locked out" by virtue of not being allowed to use their land. The only difference is: the property owner is not compensated for incurred losses as guaranteed by the Fifth Amendment.

It's all about control.

The examples given as pertaining to the Fish and Wildlife Service (FWS) can be applied to all the regulating agencies—the Corps of Engineers (COE), the Environmental Protection Agency (EPA), the Occupational Safety and Health Administration (OSHA), the National Park Service (NPS) and many more. Any agency—local, state or federal—which imposes regulations in the "public interest" that forbid a property owner from using his property, or decreases the value of that property, is subject to the "just compensation" clause of the Fifth Amendment. Those who do not abide by it are violating the U.S. Constitution.

Regardless, government bureaucracies are bursting at the seams with powercrats who will settle for nothing less than complete control of the nation's land and citizenry. The Internal Revenue Service inserts its "authority" into nearly every aspect of our lives. Anyone not complying with IRS mandates (regulations) usually experiences swift and unforgettable consequences. The OSHA watches and regulates virtually every industry in the country from row-crop farming to space technology, as does the EPA—which also interferes with individual citizens managing and using their own private properties. The FWS answers to no one in the execution of its single mission—to protect plant and animal species suggested as threatened or endangered, no matter the cost to economies, customs and cultures, lifestyles, civil liberties and the very foundation for freedom as guaranteed by the U.S. Constitution.

Property rights have become secondary in nature (and application) to the whims of bureaucrats. As the agencies grow and their administrators grant themselves and their regulators more power, property owners—even those on tiny city lots—face greater impingements on their God-given rights. The Secretary of the Interior, for example, may publish a few hundred pages of new regulations in the *Federal Register*, and suddenly those proposed rules are treated as *law* by agents of the Interior. No single piece of property rights legislation passed by Congress will noticeably relax the enforcement of thousands of regulations by hundreds of thousands of regulators.

The Federal Government operates on tax monies collected from citizens of the nation. Billions of dollars in tax revenue are appropriated each year for the perpetuation of the regulating agencies. To justify their annual funding, these government bureaucracies must justify their existence. Individual freedoms associated with owning and using private property are their biggest threat because "freedom" and "regulation," in this context, are antonyms. The "freedom" to manage wisely—as most property owners do and will—restricts regulation, thereby limiting (or even *eliminating*) the need for regulating agents and agencies. The perfect-case scenario, as far as the powerful bureaucracies are concerned, is to suspend the concept of private property altogether—in other words, accept Interior Secretary Babbitt's "communitarian interpretation."

A complete "land lock" would create the *need* for many regulators, even larger bureaucracies, and a very fat and powerful Federal Government. Socialistic preservationists of the environment—the Wilderness Society, the Nature Conservancy, Greenpeace, etc.—like the idea. It removes from their paths, too, the annoying obstacles presented by legally secured property rights.

Russell Jacobs suffered a complete regulatory land lock on his half-acre at Raymond, Wisconsin. Hundreds more property owners across the country are experiencing similar consequences at the hands of government officials. "Land lock" is another way of saying "feudalism" and "slavery." A united message from millions of landowners and hundreds of property rights organizations echoing loudly through the halls of Congress would help head off the push for complete regulatory land lock within this nation. The preservation of basic tenets of freedom *is* in the "public interest."

Conversely, the consequences for public apathy are unacceptable.

The Defeat of Prop 300

"The right to property being inviolable and sacred, no one ought to be deprived of it except in cases of evident public necessity legally ascertained, and on condition of a previous just indemnity."

—French National Assembly
"Declaration of the Rights of Men," 1789

One environmentalist wrote, "No one actually owns property. We're only stewards of it for a short time. Then we pass on and someone else takes over."[11]

Peter Berle of the Audubon Society says, "We reject the idea of property rights."

Brock Evans, who lobbies for pro-environment, anti-property interests, asserts that *all* land should "be in the public domain." He adds, "Let's take it all back."

The words and actions of eco-preservationists and government regulators are reasons for concern among property rights advocates. Fear of losing all rights to private property has led to many attempts to shore up constitutional safeguards. Some have been successful and some have failed

---

11-This quote shared by syndicated columnist "Fossil Bill" Kramer, as appeared in *The Courier*, Hatch, NM, "The Angry Environmentalist: It's Time to Talk Turkey," December 8, 1994, p. 6A.

miserably. A good example of the intense desire within federal bureaucracies and eco-socialistic groups to abolish the concept of owning and managing one's own property is shown by the fight over Arizona's Proposition 300 in 1994.

It began in 1992 when the 40th Arizona Legislature passed the Arizona Private Property Protection Act. While dealing only with state agencies, the law would have forced government to assess the consequences of imposing regulations that might constitute the "taking" of private property. The state's attorney general would have been required to draft guidelines regarding compensatory "takings." The state agency contemplating the imposition of a new regulation would have been compelled to look hard at the regulation and any alternatives available, then to estimate a financial cost if a "taking" was determined and to provide "just compensation" from within its own budget.[12]

Support for the legislation came from a woman who surprised two strangers (government employees) on her property near Phoenix. Upon demanding to know their business, the woman learned the men were considering her property—the reported site of a World War II-era Italian POW camp—for development as a state park. More support came from residents of Chandler, Arizona, who were prohibited from removing the unsightly nests of cliff swallows from beneath the eves of their houses. Another 6,600 homeowners along the Salt River learned that the state land department might confiscate their properties if the

---

12-The Private Property Protection Act of 1992, Arizona Senate Bill 1053.

river was found to have been "navigable" on the day statehood was achieved.

Only 17 percent of the land area in Arizona is privately owned. The rest is "owned" by government—The Bureau of Land Management (BLM), the U.S. Forest Service, an assortment of Native American "nations," the National Park Service (NPS), the Arizona State Land Department, etc. With the ever-growing likelihood of further encroachment on private property, landowners and commerce advocates joined most state legislators in supporting passage and the governor's signing of the Private Property Protection Act.

The entire effort was seen as a major threat to environmental and bureaucratic control of property owners. It was a challenge that had to be answered with such ferocity and effectiveness that other state legislatures would be dissuaded from attempting any similar action. Opponents of the law launched a massive campaign of confusion and misinformation upon the people of Arizona.

Left-wing environmentalists—using the misnomer "Take Back Our Rights" to bolster their own credibility—spread out rapidly across the state, collecting petition signatures to force a referendum on the 1994 General Election ballot. Their most common ploy was "informing" voters outside shopping malls and post offices that the Arizona legislature had just "repealed every anti-pollution law on the books." Then they would ask for signatures on their petitions.

They collected the necessary valid signatures. About two dozen other states had followed Arizona's lead in property rights protection. A precedent for state-by-state protection of property rights was a frightening prospect for regulation mongers. Environmental groups from across the nation descended on Arizona with a vengeance. They brought with them their vast financial resources, amassing a war chest of more than $3,000,000 to fight Prop 300.

Some national environmental organizations on record opposing private property protection legislation include the Center for Marine Conservation, Defenders of Wildlife, the Environmental Action Foundation, Friends of the Earth, Greenpeace USA, Inc., the League of Conservation Voters, the National Parks and Conservation Association, the National Wildlife Federation, the Wilderness Society and Zero Population Growth—all located in *Washington, D.C.!* Others hail from *California* and *New York*—the Sierra Club and the National Audubon Society, respectively. A minimum amount of opposition to Prop 300 originated from *within* Arizona.

Secretary of the Interior Bruce Babbitt symbolized the negative response from big government when he said the measure would "put a halt to all water management in Arizona." Babbitt's friends in government and the environmental community joined in the campaign to convince metropolitan voters that government *must not* be encumbered with complicated private property concerns because trained federal regulators know better how to manage the land than any individual citizen.

The issue again had become one of *control.* Supporters of Prop 300 fought to minimize government interference in the private actions of property owners, and opponents battled to maintain (and increase) government regulation over private land and citizens. A group called

"Arizonans for Private Property Rights" formed in support of the Proposition and mustered a budget of about $300,000—one-tenth that of the opposition.

The campaign revolved furiously around an axis of propaganda generated by the well-funded environmental groups. Opponents said, "Prop 300 will drain the state's budget." However, an independent and nonpartisan review of the Private Property Protection Act determined there would be no negative fiscal impact. Detractors said it would hurt the environment when, in fact, Prop 300 did not weaken or overturn a single environmental law already on the books. Opponents alleged that passage of Prop 300 would raise taxes and negatively affect school funding. (Ironically, revenue for schools comes directly from taxes on property.) The doomsayers charged that the law would serve "special interests"—forgetting for the moment, of course, where their own funding for this campaign was coming from. Worst of the lies, perhaps, was the recharged allegation that polluters would be "paid not to pollute."

Property-use and zoning attorney Jay Dushoff said in support of Proposition 300, "If the facts are against you, argue the law. If the law is against you, argue the facts. If the facts *and* the law are against you, yell a lot. That is what the Sierra Club and the environmental groups are doing."

And they did it well. Metropolitan and suburban voters, as well as many rural residents, fell victim to the bullets of deception fired relentlessly from the anti-property rights camp. Prop 300 failed at the polls by a margin of 60-to-40 percent. The voters of Arizona had been duped by the socialistic advocates of total "land lock" into rejecting a measure that would have reinforced the Fifth Amendment and reaffirmed the God-given sanctity of property.

Fifteen other states *did* enact various forms of property protection after 1992, some of them cut from the Arizona mold. Utah took the process a step further, applying the Arizona model to *local* governments. The protection laws simply require government to look before leaping with new regulations that might result in a "taking." Health, safety and environmental safeguards have not suffered in the states where property enjoys an added buffer of protection. The coffers of state and local governments in Utah have not been drained as a result.

The property rights issue is not dead in Arizona. Early in 1995 the Arizona legislature arranged the appointment of a "private property ombudsman." His job is to represent property owners with claims against state agencies that make new rules adversely affecting the use or value of property.

Government agencies and environmental groups that find private property rights obstructive to their respective agendas will not give up either. Battles similar to that fought in Arizona have been waged elsewhere before and they will occur again. When they do, the same envirosocialist organizations will rally against the cause of freedom. The same frightful and misleading propaganda will be touted as factual information. The same government bureaucrats will cry foul and scramble to defend their purposes. Some efforts will be won by property rights supporters, and some—like Arizona's Prop 300—will be lost.

The lost ones threaten the fabric of our free nation. Each failure—no matter how small—represents a chip from the foundation of civil liberty and freedom. The Founding

Fathers believed property rights to be sacred, equal in scope and value to the sacred rights to life and liberty. Upon the constitutional promise of secure property rights they built the most successful system of republican government and capitalistic free enterprise ever experienced in the history of the world. They recognized that perpetuating the principles of free speech and worship, due process and equal protection under the law, personal security and the unalienable pursuit of happiness, was possible only by the preservation of property.

Property must be secured or liberty cannot exist.

Just as the sanctity of property is fouled by bureaucratic regulation, extreme eco-socialistic preservationism and Supreme Court meddling, so is the future viability of the United States of America.

Staking Claim

to a Nation

A Little Bridge at Solomon

"Government is not reason, it is not eloquence—it is force!
Like fire, it is a dangerous servant and a fearful master."
—George Washington
1st U.S. President

The enemies of capitalism and free enterprise are ruthless and relentless. During the last decades of the 20th century, an evolved brand of socialist politics—practiced freely in the American Congress and courts—whittled eagerly at the vestiges of fundamental civil rights. Property once considered sacred by the founders of a nation became wantonly coveted by those who lusted for power and control. Legitimate property *owners* fought to retain meager remnants of their God-given rights. Environmentalism became the new "religion."

Extreme environmentalism feeds from the trough of socialism. The Wilderness Society, for instance, was founded by Robert Marshall, a member of the Socialist Party of Norman Thomas, and by Benton MacKaye, who belonged to the Socialist Party of America. Both were adamant foes of capitalism and private property. Greenpeace USA is another in a long list of "green" organizations that espouse socialism as the preferred alternative over entrepreneurialism and the free market system.

Greenpeace Executive Director Peter Bahouth declared, "I don't believe in the market approach . . . When companies have a bottom line of profit you won't find them thinking about the environment."[13]

Lester Brown, president of the Worldwatch Institute wrote, "Building an environmentally sustainable future requires restricting the global economy, dramatically changing human reproductive behavior, and altering values and lifestyles."[14]

Judy Bari of the militant eco-group Earth First! echoed those philosophies. "I think if we don't overthrow capitalism, we don't have a chance of saving the world ecologically. I think it is possible to have an ecologically sound society under socialism. I don't think it's possible under capitalism."[15]

Ron Arnold of the Center for the Defense of Free Enterprise says many powerful groups within the environmental movement fall "decisively in a Radical Eco-Socialist Axis."[16] They oppose the "Creator-endowed" rights of free Americans participating in the processes of free enterprise and self-management. The groups themselves

---

13-*Trashing the Economy* (footnote 7), pp. 299, 173.

14-*World Without Borders*, Lester Brown, Vintage Books, New York, NY, 1972.

15-*State Journal-Register,* Springfield, Illinois, Thursday edition, June 25, 1992.

16-*Trashing the Economy,* p. 174.

do not have the means—politically or legally—to lock up industry, private property and the multiple uses of public lands (all essential to capitalism). Therefore, they must align themselves with powerful political entities who share similar philosophies (most of the regulatory bureaucracies), or those who will chase large dangling carrots (elected officials who depend on campaign contributions). Socialist agendas of the major environmental groups—boasting millions of members (most of whom are unaware)—become endorsed and enforced by unelected regulators in government, by new "feel-good" legislation and by Supreme Court interpretation.

It's all about control. A system of true capitalism (free enterprise) requires *freedom from* control—individuals making sound management decisions based on ingenuity, productivity and competition. A system of socialism, on the other hand, demands *total control of* resources and productivity. *All* land—private and public—and the resources on it must be controlled by government. The phenomenon of "land lock," then, cannot be confined to *private* property; it must include all property.

And so we come to the story of a tiny bridge over the Gila River at Solomon, Arizona. This incredible story does not focus on a single property owner suffering property rights abuses at the hands of government regulators. It *does* focus on an entire community of property owners affected by the indifference and arrogance of government bureaucrats. Indeed, efforts to repair the flood-damaged crossing became so entangled in bureaucratic rep tape that even President Clinton was asked to intervene.

The Gila River snakes westward across southern Arizona to the Colorado River just east of Yuma. A hundred miles from its rugged wilderness headwaters in southwestern New Mexico, the Gila flows past Solomon, Arizona—a community of a few hundred people at the head of the fertile Gila Valley. Mormon farmers built several towns along this 30-mile-long stretch of river during the 1870s.

The river is a typical desert tributary. It carries snowmelt from neighboring mountains and runoff from torrential storms. It is the lifeblood for agriculture during the growing seasons. In the heat of summer some parts of it dry up as its tenuous current is drawn underground. Sometimes prolonged winter rains turn the whimsical waterway into a raging monster crashing out of the upland canyons, consuming everything in its path. Under these assaults of nature, bridges and irrigation facilities are among the first casualties.

Records show that the Gila River tends to produce a 100-year flood almost every five years. In the two decades after 1965 the Upper Gila incurred nine state declarations of emergency, five of which resulted in presidential declarations of disaster, due to flooding. In the early 1970s, Congress approved an upstream flood-control dam. Work began on the project. Almost as suddenly a lawsuit filed by the Sierra Club Legal Defense Fund shut it down. Although cost of building the dam was projected to be $9,000,000, as compared with actual flood-repair costs (between 1965 and 1985) of *$300,000,000*, the project never resumed.

Meanwhile, beginning in 1982, the Arizona Game and Fish Department attempted several times to "reintroduce" a rare species of fish—the razorback sucker—into the same stretch of river. Some research showed that the razorback had perhaps inhabited the Gila River early in the 20th century. Efforts to reintroduce the suckerfish into its "native" waters were never widely publicized and went virtually unnoticed by the residents of Graham County.

Agriculture is the largest private-sector economic contributor in Graham County, where less than seven percent of the land is privately owned. (The rest is "owned" or managed by government.) Farming represents 30 percent of the total economic base—about $30,000,000—and 20 percent of the work force. In 1994, farmers along the Gila River irrigated 33,000 acres, raising mostly cotton. However, 24,000 acres of this private farmland lie within the 100-year flood plain. In other words, about every five years 72 percent of the county's farmland is inundated, eroded and damaged in other ways by major flooding.

Farmers, at one time, could do stream channelization and bank stabilization work before and after flood events to reduce erosion and crop loss. However, individual landowners lost their rights to sensibly manage streamside properties when federal agencies like the Corps of Engineers and the Fish and Wildlife Service became administrators of environmental legislation. Similarly, local governments lost the ability to act in the best interest of area residents in events of natural disaster. Zealous enforcement of the Clean Water Act, the Endangered Species Act and "critical habitat" designations has resulted in virtual "lock downs" of land, resources and regional economies.

This is the way it happened in Graham County after a devastating flood on the Gila River in January of 1993. When the floodwater receded, hundreds of acres of private farmland along the river were gone. Tons of debris lay strewn about remaining cottonfields. Irrigation diversions and canals had crumbled. And an 86-foot-long concrete bridge at Solomon stood like an old monument in some forgotten graveyard, its long earthen ramps cut through and carried away by the raging currents. Forty-one families on the north side of the river were now isolated from their own fields on the south bank, as well as from their post office and school. What once had been a short jaunt over the river for schoolbuses and cumbersome farm equipment now became a 28-mile-long round trip through Safford—the county seat (with a much higher population density) several miles downstream.

Graham County officials recognized that the safety and economic well-being of many local residents would be affected by any prolonged delay in reopening a crossing at Solomon. The project became one of many in a recovery effort that spanned the county. Not long after the 1993 flood, county planners had identified several funding sources totaling $2,000,000 for the design, engineering and construction of a new *400-foot-long* structure to replace the old 86-foot span. The new bridge would reach nearly from bank to bank, eliminating the long earthen approaches and future washouts. In May, the county channeled the river back under the old bridge and installed a temporary minimal-service crossing. The Arizona Department of Transportation (ADOT) assumed the role of "lead agency" in the upcoming project. In August, a consulting engineer began work on the new bridge design. A month later, county officials contacted the Corps of Engineers about location of the high water mark at the site. The project seemed to be progressing smoothly.

Then the U.S. Fish and Wildlife Service proposed the Upper Gila River as "critical habitat" for the protection of the endangered razorback sucker. When a critical habitat is *proposed*—just as when a species is *proposed* for listing as endangered—management (federal regulation) takes over as if the *proposal* is a *designation*. The Solomon Bridge project stopped in its tracks, subject to bureaucratic scrutiny and manipulation. In March of 1994, the formal "critical habitat designation" appeared in the *Federal Register* and FWS took full control of the river.

Every other agency of state and federal government involved in this project must now consult with FWS. The process for obtaining a Section 404 permit under the Clean Water Act from the Corps of Engineers was put on hold pending FWS review. In the same month that habitat designation occurred, Graham County made a recommendation to ADOT on bridge alignment and the COE compiled a map of the Gila River "ordinary high water mark." A month later, a "Preliminary Hydraulic Report" and a "Draft Environmental Analysis" were submitted to ADOT. The "Preliminary [Bridge] Design Report" followed in May.

And nothing happened. No one could move forward with any part of the project without review, comment and approval by FWS. Time passed. High water from summer storms washed out the temporary crossing. Again, families were isolated on the north side of the Gila. Accelerated erosion continued to broaden the riverbed where streambank stabilization and revegetation was forbidden in deference to a transplanted suckerfish. One farmer watched his 130-acre field on the south side of the river reduced to less than 50 acres. A 400-foot-long new bridge would no longer be adequate. County officials proposed a structure spanning 800 feet to provide a safe and reliable crossing causing a minimal impact on stream flow and conditions. Nothing happened as Graham County waited for FWS to respond.

In January of 1995, William Belt at ADOT received a letter from the U.S. Environmental Protection Agency (EPA), stating, "Based upon our review of [the project documentation], we concur that the information provided to EPA is adequate to allow the Arizona Department of Transportation to move to the next stage in the NEPA-404 integration process."

On the same day, Sam Spiller, Arizona Supervisor for the U.S. Fish and Wildlife Service, wrote to Belt, "We reviewed the 'Preliminary Design Report,' and the project purpose and need and offer the following comments for your consideration. We believe that the purpose and need statement is inadequate. Although it is not stated, we believe that the purpose of the project is to provide a safe automobile transportation facility at a general location on the Gila River. The Service believes that less damaging alternatives may exist . . . Alternatives that would not result in channel narrowing or constriction and avoid or minimize the placement of fill into Waters of the United States should be considered."

A review of Spiller's comments reveals an arrogance common at the FWS agency and among its agents. Sitting in a Phoenix office, Spiller decided the Solomon Bridge "purpose and need statement" was "inadequate," then applied his own spin to it. The "alternatives" he suggested equate to nothing less than allowing the river to rampage out of its banks and carry hundreds of acres of valuable farmland downstream. Spiller also contended in his letter that "threatened, endangered, or proposed species" might be affected, again delaying the project by suggesting "formal section 7 consultation may be required."

The U.S. Fish and Wildlife Service has no mission other than to manage for the protection of species that are listed as threatened or endangered or proposed for such listing. At one meeting Graham County Supervisor Terry Bingham asked Sam Spiller, "When do we consider *people* in this?" Spiller answered, "We don't."

Even while trying to comply with entangling regulations and the snail's-pace process of endless reviews and consultations, county officials *did*, however, have to consider people. Theirs was a *daily* consideration for the economic hardships and health and safety hazards brought by having part of the county cut in half. The Solomonville School District budget suffered the costs of an additional bus and three 28-mile round trips per day. Hundreds of acres of farmland—crucial to family livelihoods and the county tax base—were being swept away. Access to doctors and other critical services was impaired. Large tractors and cotton-pickers were forced to travel a ten-mile stretch of highway with an average daily traffic count of 17,000 instead of a short bridge over the river. Meanwhile, Sam Spiller continued to play God, refusing to approve the most obvious and reasonable of options.

On July 21, 1994, ADOT enlisted the expertise of an eco-consultant George Ruffner. Within a month Ruffner had visited the site and prepared a report favoring the bridge project. The report went to ADOT, then to the Federal Highways Administration and to FWS. Fish and Wildlife responded that "more information is needed." In September Federal Highways informed Graham County that the necessary environmental report could not be completed until the 404 permit process was essentially complete. The COE then revised the high water mark and Federal Highways said the EPA would have to come and look at it. All efforts failed to get an EPA representative to the location.

Floundering in a maze of federal bureaucracy, county officials launched an effort to obtain permission from the Corps of Engineers to do "emergency work" at the bridge location. In a letter to COE Permit Coordinator Robert Dummer, Graham County Manager Joe Carter cited the summer farming season, the threatened Solomonville School District budget and an ongoing construction project on part of the 28-mile detour route as justification for the *immediate* need for a new *temporary* crossing at Solomon. This work would include rechanneling the river back into place under the old 86-foot-long bridge and installing some culverts in a smaller side channel. The work would have been consistent with emergency recovery activity following every flood event dating back to 1972—that is, until the river became a suckerfish habitat.

After a month-long flurry of meetings and telephone conversations between Carter, Dummer, Sam Spiller and others—including Arizona Senator John McCain—John Gill, the COE's Chief of the Regulatory Branch, denied the request. He suggested a "repair design without any upstream diversion."

Throughout the remainder of 1994 Carter and the supervisors of Graham County continued to pursue every possible avenue of resolution to this seemingly unsolvable stalemate. Dialogue and correspondences traveled frequently between Graham County and the offices of COE and FWS. The prescribed processes for obtaining 404 permits continued. Every indication that COE might cooperate with the county was preempted by cursory determinations and "opinions" from dogmatic Fish and Wildlife bureaucrats like Sam Spiller.

On January 30, 1995, Joe Carter wrote to President Clinton: "We in Graham County have had a bridge closed for over two years now while the U.S. Fish and Wildlife Service, Environmental Protection Agency, and the Corps of Engineers debate its replacement and, in the case of the Fish and Wildlife Service, whether we even need it. I believe the Corps of Engineers has a genuine desire to move quickly but appears to be bogged down in consultation processes with other agencies and, perhaps, intimidated by special interest groups over environmental issues." No response.

Arizona Governor Fife Symington carried the story to the office of Speaker of the U.S. House Newt Gingrich. A polite audience but no results.

County officials asked U.S. Congressman Jim Kolbe and Senators John McCain and Dennis DeConcini to intervene for them with the federal agencies. Little response and less results.

In mid-February 1995, Arizona Speaker of the House Mark Killian appealed to Major Robert Van Der Like, Deputy Commander of the Army Corps of Engineers for Arizona and Nevada. Two weeks later Killian received a letter from the Chief of the Regulatory Branch Arizona Field Office, Cindy Lester: ". . . a substantial amount of upstream construction work, dike and channel excavation, is necessary to keep the crossing open. This work, in critical habitat for the endangered razorback sucker (*Xyrauchen texanus*), is a 'may affect' situation under the Endangered Species Act and would require formal Section 7 consultation with the U.S. Fish and Wildlife Service. Formal Section 7 consultation requires that a biological assessment be prepared and sent to the U.S. Fish and Wildlife Service to review."

Again, the FWS rules supreme. Nobody can move without jumping through bureaucratic hoops held up for the sole purpose of ensuring the unchallenged power of FWS and its eco-ingrained powercrats. Lester continues in her letter that the Section 7 process is "labor intensive and lengthy" and that the "consultation process must be completed before the Corps can permit any work, even temporary repairs, under Section 404 of the Clean Water Act."

After two years of hardship and intense effort by Graham County citizens and officials, the Solomon Bridge project still lay dead on square one—exactly where it was when the bridge washed out in January of 1993.

Joe Carter appealed to Lester on the basis of an emergency clause outlined within the Clean Water Act:

> (4) Emergency procedures. *Division engineers are authorized to approve special processing procedures in emergency situations. An "emergency" is a situation which would result in an*

> *unacceptable hazard to life, a significant loss of
> property, or an immediate, unforeseen, and
> significant economic hardship if corrective action
> requiring a permit is not undertaken within a time
> period less than the normal time needed to process
> the application under standard procedures.*

Carter argued that all the criteria were met—an unacceptable hazard to life, significant property loss and economic hardship. Lester explained the definition of an "emergency" by county government was different from that of the COE. In their eyes an emergency may exist as long as floodwater is rising, but ends when the water starts to recede.

In a special meeting on April 6, 1995, the Graham County Board of Supervisors unanimously decided to rechannel the river and install a temporary crossing without the necessary permits from the Corps of Engineers. A brisk exchange of memos and other communication between the county and the various agencies followed. The COE said it planned to issue a permit for the temporary crossing and a new 800-foot-long bridge, perhaps as early as June, but there was no guarantee. Determined to represent the best interests of the citizens of Graham County, the supervisors advertised for a contractor to do the work.

On April 13, an FWS staffer under Sam Spiller wrote a letter of panic to Cindy Lester: ". . . the Gila River in the area of the proposed work supports the endangered razorback sucker . . . the endangered Southwestern willow flycatcher . . . and the proposed endangered cactus ferruginous pygmy owl. Therefore, issuance of a section

404 permit for the proposed work must comply with section 7 of the Endangered Species Act." Ranting in desperation over the prospect of no longer wielding absolute control in this matter, the FWS cited the questionable presence of the suckerfish, a newly-listed songbird and a species of desert owl only *proposed* for listing.

Graham County hired a contractor.

The COE notified Joe Carter that the supervisors could each face administrative and punitive fines exceeding $50,000 per day and imprisonment up to three years for their actions if a temporary crossing was installed without the necessary permits. Further, the permitting process for the new bridge might be delayed.

Bulldozers entered the river on April 21. Four days later, the crossing was open to traffic.

On April 28, James Burton, Habitat Branch Chief for the Arizona Game and Fish Department, sent a letter to Cindy Lester regarding the permitting process for the new bridge. In part, he wrote: "The proposed project site occurs within the reach of the Gila River designated by the USFWS as Critical Habitat for the Endangered razorback sucker (*Xyrauchen texanus*). While the reach has been designated critical habitat, occurrence of razorback suckers within this area is very rare and, based upon current information, they are highly unlikely to inhabit the proposed project site. Attempts to reintroduce [the] razorback sucker have been made in this reach of the Gila River (during the 1980s), but have met with very limited success. We've had no recaptures within the vicinity of the project site."

On the same day, Cindy Lester wrote to Graham County Engineer Jim Moser, also about the new bridge permit: "To facilitate completion of our review of your permit application . . . you [must] include the following three items in your response: (1) A plan for a temporary crossing . . . open to traffic until the new bridge is completed; (2) A proposal to reduce upstream and downstream bank erosion problems (rechanneling); and (3) A brief discussion of what damage a large, medium, and small flood event may cause to the new bridge . . ."

On May 4, county officials received an official "Notice of Violation of the Clean Water Act" from Carl Enson, Chief of the COE's Construction-Operations Division. It read: "I am disappointed that you felt compelled to conduct this work in light of the effort my Regulatory staff has put forth to coordinate with you and expedite your application for the permanent bridge crossing . . . Your actions have served to complicate and possibly delay this decision."

Was this "notice" a bureaucratic formality? Was it an attempt to frighten or intimidate Graham County officials? No one outside the COE knows for sure. Remember, the correspondence came from the Corps of Engineers—the one federal agency that seemed to understand the problem and want to help. Interestingly, the U.S. Fish and Wildlife Service—the agency that effectively tied everyone's hands throughout the process—did not respond to the county's action in any way.

On June 19, 1995—*two and a half years after the bridge washed out at Solomon*—Graham County Manager Joe Carter released the following memo: "It is with pleasure that I notify you that the Corps of Engineers has issued a 404 permit for the new eight-hundred-foot-long Solomon bridge. The Board of Supervisors . . . [has] reviewed its provisions and authorized the permit to be signed. In short, [this] action will close the enforcement proceedings initiated by the Corps in their Notice of Violation letter dated May 1, 1995 . . ."[17]

The county got its permit. The same document gave permission to maintain the temporary crossing during the bridge construction process. County supervisors were not fined or sent to jail for taking hard action in the interest of their constituents. The Solomon crossing, with channelization and streambank revegetation, will change from a flood-torn wasteland to an exemplary riparian area.

So why the two-and-a-half-year delay? Why the economic hardship on the families and taxpayers of the county? Why the maddening, endless processes of memorandums and assessments, consultations, applications, reviews and requests for more information, more agencies inviting their own participation, more studies and the string of cursory denials, refusals, disapprovals and rejections? Why the interference from high-handed bureaucrats who do not live there and, in many cases, never came to the project site? We are not talking about authorizing and building a new major dam or open-pit copper mine where the landscape and geography will be forever changed. We are

---

17-Details of the Solomon Bridge story, whether written here or omitted in the interest of brevity, are contained in copies of the letters, memos and other correspondence specified in the text, all of which are preserved in the author's files.

talking about *replacing* a flood-damaged river crossing that has existed for over half a century!

It's all about control—government control of people and "special-interest" control of government. The regulatory agencies (most especially FWS) have become sanctuaries for socialistic-minded envirocrats and radical preservationists. Perhaps the one thing that frightens eco-charged bureaucracies more than a property owner managing his own land is a whole county governing itself. When they are out of the loop, they are no longer important. Without importance there is no power. And with no power there is no need for them to exist. In the spirit of self-preservation, bureaucrats strive tirelessly to control that which they fear most.

Never let it be thought that FWS accepts defeat gracefully. As engineering and design work resumed on the Solomon Bridge project, federal agents busied themselves scouring the banks of the Gila River. In June 1995, they *claimed* to have located an active nest of endangered southwestern willow flycatchers in the path of the bridge alignment. County officials were not allowed to see the nest because federal law prohibits disclosure of site-specific information on endangered species. FWS initiated consultation between the agencies again! Among their recommended options: a proposal to "mitigate" for a single nest by taking control of 15 miles of riverside flood plain—*including hundreds of acres of private property!*—for possible so-called "habitat rehabilitation."

Senator Jon Kyl—who came to the Senate with the 104th Congress in 1995—visited the Solomon Bridge site before installation of the temporary crossing. He returned to

Washington so incredulous that, in late June, he nominated the entire bridge fiasco for the annual Congressional Red Tape Award. About the nomination he said, "The Solomon Bridge story is about a rural county . . . and its battle with federal environmental regulations. The villain of this story is the Endangered Species Act, and its interpretation and enforcement by the Fish and Wildlife Service."[18]

Forty miles upstream from Solomon in Greenlee County, the Gila River flows near a town called Duncan (pop. 700). Mayor Elizabeth Tea says when the Duncan Bridge was built in 1948 "there was enough room under the bridge to fly a small aircraft" through it. "Now there is so much . . . debris that there is nowhere for the water to flow except over the banks and into [town] . . . Every flood just causes the [river]bed to become higher and is now higher than our town." Tea blames the Environmental Protection Agency and the Endangered Species Act (U.S. Fish and Wildlife Service) for the town of Duncan "dying a little more each year because we are unable to work on the dike that protects our town."

Duncan, Arizona, does not have the resources or the personnel to fight as hard or as long as Graham County. An air of hopelessness abides there. It's one of hundreds—even thousands—of small towns across rural America that struggle in the chokehold of government regulation. It's also one of the reasons the Solomon Bridge drama did not receive the Red Tape Award. Similar stories abound elsewhere. In fact, the Red Tape Award for 1995 went to

---

18-*Eastern Arizona Courier*, Wednesday, July 5, 1995, Section 1, p. 1.

"past Congresses" in recognition of their "knack for overburdening American citizens."

When Arizona's Governor Symington suggested scrapping the Endangered Species Act in early 1995, eco-preservationists across the country were horrified. Rob Smith of the Sierra Club says the ESA is "one of the strongest and best environmental acts we have." Like-minded Interior Secretary Bruce Babbitt emphasizes the ESA is ". . . the most important . . . the most ingenious . . . piece of environmental legislation ever conceived."

The bureaucrats and eco-socialists *say* they are protecting the environment. The citizens of Graham County and Duncan, Arizona, however, know that words like "strongest" and "ingenious," used in this context, describe the ability of government, acting under the color of "law," to *control* the land and its people.

Telescopes, Squirrels and Apaches

"The property which every man has in his own labor, as it is the original foundation of all other property, so it is the most sacred and inviolable."

—Adam Smith
English philosopher, 1776

Land lock is not unique to private property. While thousands of private landowners endure the egregious offenses of dogmatic bureaucrats, the users of unappropriated federal lands find themselves facing hundreds of new regulations each year designed especially to make land use more difficult. Traditional uses of these nonprivate lands include cattle grazing and mining, timber harvest, gas and oil exploration and production and recreation. Government agencies seem determined to end all public use of the so-called "public lands." As ghostly monuments to the effort, some small towns in the West sit boarded up and deserted where families once lived and worked, worshiped and sent their children to school. These are ghost towns of the *New* West—abandoned in the *1990s*. Their economies were built on the management and harvest of resources. Socialistic envirocrats like Interior Secretary Bruce Babbitt, however, believe that only big government agencies are capable of managing those resources—and the agencies have become overrun with diehard preservationists. The term "manage" now means "control" —*total* control.

Just as government bureaucracies work to carry out the stratagem of "land lock" through overzealous enforcement of environmental laws, so do the preservationist groups through courtroom maneuvers and media hysteria. Nowhere is the intent more apparent than at the University of Arizona's Mt. Graham International Observatory project.

Mt. Graham rises to 10,720 feet above sea level very near the center of the magnificent 300-square-mile Pinaleno (Peen-uh-layn'-yoh) Range in southeastern Arizona. The so-called "sky island"[19] has been the location for a variety of events throughout history. It was named in 1846 by a topographical engineer on a western mapping expedition. It was a sanctuary for outlaws and renegade Apaches. Pioneer loggers harvested timber during the late 1800s, supplying several sawmills with raw material for lumber production. Mexican bandits are believed to have buried their plunder there. The mountain served as one of several heliograph stations from which Morse code messages were transmitted from sky island to sky island as the U.S. Army tracked the elusive Geronimo. Early settlers raised potatoes in the high meadows. A U.S. Cavalry infirmary and a project of the Civilian Conservation Corps (CCC) were headquartered there.

Today Mt. Graham is a part of the Coronado National Forest. Visitors travel State Route 366 to designated camping and picnicking areas like Treasure Park, Soldier Creek and Riggs Flat Lake. The roadway ascends through five distinctive ecological planes in a span of 20 miles, leaving desert greasewoods and prickly pears, passing through alligator juniper and manzanita groves to high forests of evergreens and aspens.

In the early 1980s, Mt. Graham became the focal point for a new community of explorers—the University of Arizona (renowned for its astronomy program), the Vatican Observatory in Italy, the Max Planck Institute of Germany

---

19-So named because isolated mountains near the southern tip of the Rocky Mountain chain jut out of the high desert floor like islands in a sea, with no apparent link to neighboring mountains.

and other smaller partners. The astronomers were seeking the most ideal site for a series of advanced-technology land-based telescopes. They rated 280 mountaintops exceeding 9,000 feet in elevation. Important criteria included altitude, low humidity, absence of cloud cover, absence of light pollution and proximity to an existing astronomical facility.

The scientists selected Mt. Graham. The site shared many necessary characteristics with other potential sites and offered some bonuses as well. A paved road already traversed the mountainside almost to its summit. Historic Heliograph Peak had been developed as a site for commercial communications towers and a fire lookout tower. Other development included campsites, picnic grounds, hiking trails, horse corrals, private summer cabins, a church camp and two manmade lakes. About 10,000 acres in the range had been logged and reforested in the 60 years preceding 1980. More than 150 years of human activity seemed to have been absorbed naturally within the immense landscape.

Over the objections of some mainstream environmental organizations, the U.S. Congress passed the Arizona Wilderness Act of 1984. The legislation designated 3,500 acres as a potential astrophysical research study area in the Pinaleno Range. University scientists began working with federal and state agencies to prepare the necessary biological assessments (*two* of them by the U.S. Forest Service) and biological opinions (*two* of them by the U.S. Fish and Wildlife Service) and an environmental impact statement. The agencies conducted a series of public hearings and comment periods. Public relations officials at the University of Arizona sent letters of intent to more than

20 Native American tribes, requesting their participation on the proposed observatory project. Those located nearest to the project were contacted twice.

The preliminary work took four years. During that time no effort was spared to minimize the impact of inserting an astrophysical observatory into the mountain environment. When the residents of surrounding communities learned they would never see hulking telescope domes cluttering the top of "their mountain," and that placing scopes there would not terminate public access, they voiced overwhelming support. The largest town in the county replaced its mercury-vapor street lights with sodium-vapor fixtures to reduce light pollution. No response—negative or positive—came from any Native American group.

The preservationists were digging in. The Sierra Club vowed to fight development of the observatory. Eco-radicals came from every direction to join the foray. The Arizona Wildlife Federation rose up in anger. Ultra eco-preservationist Dr. Robin Silver expressed outrage over Congress and the University of Arizona conspiring to destroy another piece of Eden. The militant group Earth First! rallied around the cause.

A small species of red squirrel living near the project site became their chariot. They proposed the rodent for listing as endangered. The proposal came with very little scientific data. Biologists agreed summarily that thousands of years of isolation at the top of Mt. Graham *probably* caused this squirrel to differ slightly from red squirrels in the White Mountains and Kaibab National Forest of Arizona. Biologists said the "unique subspecies" was set apart, not by its characteristics, but by its behavior. The Mt. Graham red squirrel (*Tamiasciurus hudsonicus grahamensis*) had been categorized as a *game* animal by the Arizona Game and Fish Department until 1986. Due to an intense campaign by determined preservationists, it was listed as "endangered" by FWS in 1987.

Parameters for the project changed forever. The preservationists had just attained a chokehold they would never relax.

The University cut its plan for 18 telescopes to seven, confined to two peaks. University planners and federal agents reduced the plan even further in 1988. The observatory would be built in two stages—on *one* peak. It would cost an estimated $200,000,000.

Congress enacted the Arizona-Idaho Conservation Act (AICA) of 1988, incorporating the terms of the FWS Biological Opinion agreed to by the Forest Service and the University. The AICA designated 1,700 acres surrounding the observatory site as a protected "refugium" for the red squirrels. The law authorized the University and its partners to build *three* telescopes and an access road to the site. Four additional scopes would be considered only after extensive monitoring of squirrels by FWS turned up no adverse effects brought on by the presence of scopes and humankind.

The entire project could occupy no more than 24 acres (including roadway), and the first three scopes must be contained within 8.6 acres. A two-mile-long access road would consume more than six of those acres. Individually, one telescope would occupy a quarter-acre site, another would take up one-third of an acre and the third (planned to be the most powerful land-based telescope in the world) would sit on 1.2 acres. So the 3,500-acre "astrophysical research study area" was now reduced to less than nine acres of actual project site in the middle of 12,000 acres of Mt. Graham red squirrel habitat.

Further, the AICA required the University to commit at least $100,000 per year to monitoring the red squirrels. The study period would run ten years. (From 1988 to 1994, the University averaged more than twice that amount on squirrel monitoring.) Compliance with every congressional stipulation was achieved. Cooperation between the University, its partners and the administrative agencies of federal government (Forest Service and FWS) seemed optimum. Construction work on the first telescope began in the spring of 1989.

But it's not a perfect world. Anti-development eco-radicals were not ready to let this association between land users and managing agencies proceed smoothly. The Sierra Club Legal Defense Fund filed a nine-claim lawsuit against the Forest Service and the FWS. It named the Mt. Graham red squirrel as a plaintiff. The suit contended that construction of the observatory would lead to extinction of the subspecies. An endless tide of litigation procedures would follow. The tenacity of the preservationists is illustrated in a partial chronology of their legal maneuvering:

June 21, 1989: A complaint listing nine claims was filed against U.S. Forest Service and U.S. Fish and Wildlife Service by Sierra Club, et al, for declaratory and injunctive relief in Washington, D.C.

July 20, 1989: Sierra Club voluntarily dismissed the Washington, D.C., lawsuit without prejudice.

July 27, 1989: The same complaint listing nine claims was filed against U.S. Forest Service and U.S. Fish and Wildlife Service by Sierra Club, et al, for declaratory and injunctive relief in Federal District Court in Tucson, AZ.

August 22, 1989: Sierra Club filed a motion for preliminary injunction precluding construction of the access road.

August 30, 1989: Sierra Club motion denied by Court.

August 31, 1989: Sierra Club appealed denial of request for preliminary injunction to the Ninth U.S. Circuit Court of Appeals.

September 6, 1989: Sierra Club filed emergency motion for injunction pending appeal before the Ninth Circuit Court.

September 15, 1989: Sierra Club motion denied.

November 13, 1989: Sierra Club filed emergency motion for reconsideration of the order granting the stay of injunction pending appeal.

November 20, 1989: Sierra Club motion denied.

November 27, 1989: Federal Judge Alfredo Marquez held an evidentiary hearing on Sierra Club's motion for preliminary injunction.

March 26, 1990: Judge Marquez ordered a 120-day injunction on construction work to allow Congress time to review their own AICA legislation.

May 15, 1990: Ninth Circuit Court granted the AZ Board of Regents a stay of the 120-day injunction, allowing construction work to proceed.

May 26, 1990: Sierra Club filed motion for reconsideration of the order granting the stay of injunction pending appeal.

June 4, 1990: Federal District Court dismissed seven of the nine claims listed in the July 27, 1989, Sierra Club complaint.

June 12, 1990: Sierra Club appealed the District Court judgment to the Ninth Circuit.

June 26, 1990: Sierra Club motion for reconsideration of stay of 120-day injunction denied.

June 28, 1990: Sierra Club filed motion for continuance pending outcome of a "biological update."

July 3, 1990: Sierra Club motion denied.

July 10, 1990: Sierra Club filed motion regarding the remaining two claims from the July 27, 1989, complaint to stay the litigation or dismiss without prejudice; motion to stay the litigation was granted by Judge Marquez.

July 18, 1990: Sierra Club withdrew the appeal of dismissal of first seven claims in the July 27, 1989, complaint from before the Ninth Circuit Court.

August 2, 1990: Sierra Club refiled the same appeal of the dismissal of the first seven claims before the Ninth Circuit Court.

August 27, 1990: Sierra Club filed motion in District Court for a temporary restraining order, preliminary injunction hearing and for injunction pending appeal based on reconsultation claims.

August 28, 1990: Sierra Club motion denied.

September 4, 1990: Sierra Club filed emergency motion for an injunction pending appeal based upon reconsultation claims before the Ninth Circuit Court.

September 18, 1990: Ninth Circuit Court consolidated all three Sierra Club appeals and granted an injunction pending appeal.

September 28, 1990: Ninth Circuit Court reversed the order for injunction pending appeal.

October 1, 1990: Sierra Club filed emergency petition for rehearing before the Ninth Circuit; petition was denied.

December 13, 1990: Ninth Circuit Court held hearing of consolidated Sierra Club appeals.

April 9, 1991: Ninth Circuit Court remanded to the District Court for evidentiary hearing on the Sierra Club's claim that the red squirrel monitoring program was inadequate, and ordered Sierra Club to file an application for a temporary restraining order.

April 16, 1991: Sierra Club filed application for a temporary restraining order and filed a motion for a preliminary injunction.

May 17, 1991: District Court ruled that the monitoring program was adequate and denied petition for a temporary restraining order.

Meanwhile, the access road to the observatory site was completed and work had started on the second telescope. But progress was slow and often interrupted by injunctions and pending appeals. Biologists reported an *increase* in the number of red squirrels. These same observers reported most of the "unique subspecies" was living at lower altitudes of the mixed conifer zone—*away* from the construction project. Militant Earth First!ers gathered on the mountain periodically to block roads and chain themselves to construction equipment.

The objective of Sierra Club and other opponents of the project was clearly something other than protecting squirrels. The endless barrage of court filings had failed to stop the project or to lock up the mountain. The red squirrel "cause" was not working. A new stratagem must be found—perhaps a more controversial issue. A sensitive and emotional debate involving *people*—not rodents—might stop this congressionally approved project. Why not?

The same opponents who expended the red squirrel issue created a Tucson-based group and named it the "Apache Survival Coalition." They recruited some Native American activists, but the coalition was comprised mostly of the same non-Indian preservationists involved in the Sierra Club lawsuits. Presently the issue of ancient religion came up and Mt. Graham was identified as a sacred shrine. The group sued the Forest Service for desecrating their holy place of worship.

The San Carlos Apache Reservation lies within 25 miles of Mt. Graham. However, San Carlos officials have shunned representation by, participation in and specific claims made through the Apache Survival Coalition. In early 1993 several members of the San Carlos Tribe traveled to Europe to dispel negative propaganda being peddled to Vatican and Max Planck Institute officials. Later in the year, San Carlos Tribal Chairman Harrison Talgo and most members of the Tribal Council visited the observatory site and voiced support and enthusiasm for the project.

Some tribal members at San Carlos sincerely believe *some* areas of the Pinaleno Mountains are sacred. Most have no opinion. University of Arizona officials have worked closely with the tribe to address their concerns. They have formed partnerships in areas of education, agriculture and economic development.

Opponents of the Mt. Graham International Observatory again sought to control (kill) the project through litigation. The legal onslaught continued:

August 19, 1991: The Apache Survival Coalition filed complaint in Federal District Court in Phoenix seeking withdrawal of Special Use Permit, preliminary and permanent injunctions stopping construction, and an order requiring compliance with applicable federal laws.

October 16, 1991: District Court denied Sierra Club's motion for preliminary injunction and ruled in favor of the AZ Board of Regents on the remaining two claims in the July 27, 1989, Sierra Club complaint.

October 31, 1991: Sierra Club requested reconsideration of District Court decision in favor of Regents.

November 15, 1991: Sierra Club request for reconsideration denied.

December 11, 1991: Ninth Circuit Court ruled on consolidated appeals in favor of the Mt. Graham International Observatory: no further consultation of federal agencies is required prior to construction of first three telescopes; The Arizona-Idaho Conservation Act (AICA) was intended by Congress to balance astrophysical and biological interests.

February 10, 1992: Apache Survival Coalition filed motion for partial summary judgment on the grounds that Title VI of the AICA violates the U.S. Constitution.

March 30, 1992: U.S. Forest Service and AZ Board of

Regents filed motion for summary judgment and requested that all motions for summary judgment and the motion of the Apache Survival Coalition for partial summary judgment be heard together on June 5, 1992.

April 9, 1992: District Court held hearing on Apache Survival Coalition motions for temporary restraining order and preliminary injunction.

April 10, 1992: Apache Survival Coalition motions denied.

April 15, 1992: Apache Survival Coalition appealed the District Court's denial of injunction and restraining order to the Ninth Circuit Court.

May 6, 1992: District Court denied Apache Survival Coalition's request for additional discovery, including an on-site inspection.

May 27, 1992: District Court denied Apache Survival Coalition motion for partial summary judgment and granted Forest Service and Regents' motions for summary judgment in favor of federal defendants and the University.

July 1, 1992: Apache Survival Coalition appealed District Court's rulings in favor of federal defendants and University.

October 5, 1992: Oral arguments before Ninth Circuit Court on Sierra Club's second appeal regarding the adequacy of the squirrel monitoring program.

March 3, 1993: Ninth Circuit again found squirrel monitoring adequate and denied Sierra Club's second appeal (end of Sierra Club/red squirrel litigation).

August 31, 1993: Oral arguments before Ninth Circuit Court on Apache Survival Coalition's consolidated appeal.

April 8, 1994: Ninth Circuit found the AICA to be constitutional and the Apaches' objections to the project were brought only after an "inexcusable delay" (end of Apache Survival Coalition litigation).

At this point, both squirrels and ancient religion had been used as "surrogates" in the preservationists' fight to prevent the construction of telescopes on Mt. Graham. The issue was never about saving a species of rodent or old-growth trees or sacred shrines. It was about control. The Sierra Club revealed the true nature of its opposition in 1993 when the University proposed locating the third telescope about a half-mile from the other two. By changing sites, construction would require the removal of fewer trees and no squirrel middens (food caches) would be disturbed. Forest Service and FWS officials approved the new site as a preferred location. Nevertheless, the environmentalists *objected!*

The Mt. Graham Coalition—made up of Sierra Club, Dr. Robin Silver, Greater Gila Biodiversity Project and a dozen or so more groups and eco-radicals—sprang to life. A new legal assault began:

May 25, 1994: Mt. Graham Coalition filed suit against the U.S. Forest Service in Washington, D.C., alleging location of the third telescope to be improper.

June 10, 1994: The AZ Board of Regents intervened in Washington, D.C..

June 16, 1994: Mt. Graham Coalition transferred its lawsuit to Arizona Federal District Court in Tucson.

July 2, 1994: District Court entered a temporary restraining order prohibiting any further work at the telescope site.

July 25, 1994: All parties filed motions for summary judgment.

July 28, 1994: District Court entered a permanent injunction against further work on the third telescope pending exhaustive new environmental studies.

August 1, 1994: Regents appealed to Ninth Circuit asking for stay of District Court order pending appeal and filed motion requesting stay of District Court's injunction pending appeal.

August 24, 1994: Regents' motion denied; appeal expedited and oral argument set for November.

September 1, 1994: Regents filed motion to modify the injunction to allow site preparation but no construction.

September 28, 1994: Regents' motion denied.

November 16, 1994: Oral argument presented in Ninth Circuit on appeal of District Court injunction.

April 27, 1995: Ninth Circuit Court upheld the District Court ruling that federal agencies did not have the authority to approve a new telescope placement location without further environmental studies.

June 8, 1995: Regents requested a rehearing of argument in the Ninth Circuit.

June 29, 1995: The U.S. Justice Department requested a rehearing.

July 26, 1995: Ninth Circuit Court denied Regents' request for rehearing.

August 4, 1995: Ninth Circuit denied U.S. Justice Department request for rehearing.

The preservationists have learned well how to control by litigation. They know the courts are overloaded with pending cases. By tirelessly repeating their motions and appeals they can stall projects like the Mt. Graham International Observatory almost indefinitely. Meanwhile, investors become weary and sometimes drop out. Litigants are forced to endure spiraling legal costs. The objective is to make the development project so difficult that it will be abandoned or taken elsewhere.

In the case of Mt. Graham, a 300-square-mile range was taken hostage by capricious lawsuits over a two-acre clearing in the trees. Since ground was broken for the first telescope, the mountain was included in a Fish and Wildlife Service critical habitat designation for the threatened Mexican spotted owl. Lawsuits began almost immediately over other uses of the mountain from campground development to forest management.

It's all about control—*total* control of the land and all resources on it. There exists an attitude among preservationists that development and resource harvest are bad practices. Due to government regulation coupled with environmental lawsuits, timber harvest has been eliminated on whole national forests. Mining companies seldom expand and almost never develop new operations. Our great capitalist nation would never have become industrialized had the same mindset prevailed early in the 20th century. There would have been no dams built, no powerlines or pipelines installed, no industrial parks or factories developed.

Supporters of the Mt. Graham Observatory (people who live near it) recognize the potential benefits of this small and isolated development on a very large mountain. Astronomy is a "clean" industry; it does not generate air, soil or water pollution. It provides jobs and attracts tourists. The people living and working in communities surrounding Mt. Graham did not file lawsuits to stop the project.

The scientific significance of this project should not be discounted. The first two telescopes were completed and put into limited use during 1994. The Vatican Advanced Technology Telescope (VATT) is a $3,000,000 instrument capable of producing extremely sharp optical and infrared images. Vatican astronomers will study stars in the process of becoming main-sequence stars like the earth's sun, perhaps forming their own planets. The Heinrich Hertz Submillimeter Telescope (SMT) is the most accurate radio telescope ever built. Modern astronomers believe the SMT will become an important tool in exploring the process of star and planet formation both within our own Milky Way galaxy and others throughout the universe. Both instruments will be shared with talented young scientists from around the world.[20]

The Large Binocular Telescope (LBT) will be the most powerful land-based optical instrument in the world. The battle goes on over its placement and construction. Congress approved the project in the Arizona-Idaho Conservation Act of 1988. The Ninth U.S. Circuit Court of Appeals reaffirmed that approval in their December 11, 1991, ruling. Undaunted Sierra Club lawyers persist in clogging the courts with reams of filings. They do not allow closure. University lawyers and local governments have appealed to Congress to redefine its original intent in the AICA. In midsummer of 1995, Arizona Senator Jon Kyl and Congressman Jim Kolbe had each expressed renewed interest in supporting the observatory project and seeing it completed.

20-Details for the Mt. Graham Observatory story are taken from letters and other correspondences, University of Arizona records, various court and government documents, all of which are preserved in the author's files.

Other possible resolutions being considered in August of 1995 included building the third telescope at the original site —where squirrel middens and more trees would be destroyed—or relocating the entire project to some other country. In the interest of science, economics and time (more than a decade has passed already), neither option is preferred. The project and its sponsors, however, have become the victims of environmental "land lock"—one of *thousands* of examples across the nation of sensible development being challenged and seriously impaired by preservation extremists. A decision to build the LBT at the original site would, at this point, almost certainly be met with another lawsuit.

The issue is not over a minuscule clearing amid the towering Douglas firs on the top of Mt. Graham. It's about locking up the land and its resources from all access and uses. Three University of Arizona scientists writing in the British scientific journal "Nature" described telescope opponents as "misguided zealots addicted to confrontation" who would "abuse environmental laws in an attempt to block a benign project."

It is interesting to note that environmentalists dedicated to the cause of *genuine* environmentalism do not share the uncompromising views of Sierra Club and its anti-development clones. One such person is Jutta Alheit, a German political scientist with the Green Party in the Bundestag. She became interested enough in the Mt. Graham controversy to travel to America and have a look for herself. Interviewed later by a German newspaper, Alheit said the accusations of construction damage were "completely absurd. This is simply [political] agitation and lies from A to Z." She ultimately recommended to her Party that it should under no circumstances become involved in opposing the telescope project. She concluded, "This is a case where the solidarity front is being used abominably."[21]

Franco Pacini, Director of the Arcetri Observatory near Florence, Italy, visited Mt. Graham early in 1995. Expressing philosophical optimism, Pacini said, "Reason will prevail because science and nature cannot go one against the other." The victims of bureaucratic and environmental "land lock" in America know that "reason" has not been a part of the equation for at least two decades.

The Resource Rush

"If we all seized the property of our neighbors and grabbed from one another what we could make use of, the bonds of human society would necessarily crumble."

—Cicero
Roman statesman (106 - 43 B.C.)

The California gold rush of 1849 is probably the best known "resource rush" of all time. Of course, there were others—Colorado, The Black Hills of Dakota, the

---

21-*Berliner Morgenpost*, "Über Potsdam schwebt das Kriegsbeil," Von Korstin Ullrich, Sunday edition, March 19, 1995, p. 4.

Klondike—all in quest of a coveted shiny metal called "gold." Tombstone, Arizona, was born from a silver strike and Morenci, Arizona, resulted from the discovery of copper. Hundreds of communities like these sprang up around the West as droves of fortune-seekers sought a personal share of the earth's wealth. Many of the towns have completely disappeared and some remain, parched and crumbling, as stubborn monuments to a bygone era. Thousands came for the riches and only a few got rich. Most of the others resorted to more practical methods of making their livings. This often involved harvesting other resources from the earth.

Not long after the first pilgrims came to the eastern shores of America, intrepid settlers began pushing westward in search of game, land, timber and other resources. There was a time in our history when Kentucky and Tennessee were considered *far* west. During the 19th century an insightful Congress passed legislation encouraging settlers to inhabit and tame the West. The Oklahoma Land Grab of 1889 was another kind of "resource rush." The Mining Law of 1872 set up a standard of rights and behavior with respect to the use of unappropriated lands for mining and mineral exploration. There were "resource rushes" for the grasslands and timber, and the Homestead Act of 1862 provided 160 acres to any settler willing to stake out a parcel and work it for five years. The rights to water on such a parcel—whether running in a stream or coaxed from beneath the ground—were a kind of insurance for the property owner against some future loss of the property (or loss of use) as imposed by government or some other interloper.

The vast resources of the West became the wealth of the nation. The mines and timberlands supplied raw materials for new and expanding towns, cities and infrastructure. The farms and ranches provided food. Waterways became the sources of hydroelectric power as the nation began to industrialize and lead the world toward the 20th century. The Federal Government formed agencies in *support* of Western development (i.e., the U.S. Forest Service charged with providing a continuous supply of lumber to meet the country's growing needs).

Then came the "environmental movement" of the late 1960s and early '70s. A grand alliance grew between eco-preservationists and government. Environmentalists suggested and Congress passed benevolent laws aimed at protecting the nation's wildlife and resources. New bureaucracies emerged to administer them. The agencies filled up with preservationists empowered as policymakers and carte blanche enforcers of their own rules. Some well-funded eco-groups evolved as powerful lobbyists while others mounted massive propaganda campaigns, drawing support in dollars and opinion from a newly "enlightened" urban public.

A brand new kind of "resource rush" began. It became the objective of the preservationists to end all private and commercial consumption of natural resources. This single-sighted commitment threatens the economies of communities and whole *states!* It also affects the supply of raw materials necessary to commerce and technology around the world.

Twelve percent of Nevada's total gross product comes from the mining industry. Miners harvested more than 6,000,000 ounces of gold there in 1990. That's 62 percent of all the gold produced in the U.S. that year, and 11 percent of the world's production. As far as community economies are concerned, mining companies *invested* $5,000,000,000 in Nevada in the five years preceding 1991. The same period saw employment in the state's mining industry climb from 6,000 jobs to 16,000 jobs. State and local taxes paid by mining companies increased from $21,000,000 in 1986 to $90,000,000 in 1991.[22]

Arizona is the number one producer of hardrock (non-fuel) minerals in the nation—especially copper. In 1994, copper provided almost 12,000 jobs in the state at an average weekly income of $782. An annual payroll of $476,000,000 becomes $515,000,000 when $39,000,000 in pension payments to retirees and dividends to Arizona investors are added. The copper industry purchased $879,000,000 in goods and services and paid $133,000,000 in taxes to state and local governments. Direct spending within the state in 1994 exceeded $1,500,000,000.[23]

Other western states from Montana to New Mexico benefit from mining operations. Tens of thousands of jobs (family livelihoods) throughout the West depend on this once-respected industry. Radical environmentalism, however, has greatly affected how the nation as a whole

---

22-These Nevada statistics were originally documented for and published in *Surviving the Second Civil War* (footnote 5).

23-Statistics obtained from the Arizona Mining Association, 2702 North Third Street, Suite 2015, Phoenix, AZ 85004.

perceives the harvest of minerals from the earth. Sierra Club propaganda has painted a picture of creeks running red with pollution near Yellowstone National Park. Open-pit mines are condemned as unhealable scars on a delicate earth. Eco-socialists maintain consistently that mining companies enjoy a free ride to enormous profits on the backs of taxpayers through government subsidies on public land. Eco-radicals like Mineral Policy Center director Phil Hocker team up with liberal lawmakers like Nick Joe Rahall of West Virginia and George Miller of California to promote a bureaucratic onslaught of the industry through restrictive legislation.

No one points out that dentists use about 300,000 ounces of gold every year, or that telephones and computers (both important tools of the preservationists) cannot function without it. No one mentions the fact that the average modern home contains 400 pounds of copper or that 40 pounds of copper go to work every time a key is turned in the ignition of an automobile. A jetliner requires 9,000 pounds of copper. A newborn child will require 1,500 pounds of copper in a lifetime to enjoy the American standard of living. It is entirely safe to say that copper contributes to the existence of every other consumer item because manufacturing and all other forms of production (farming, lumbering, fishing, food processing, etc.) depend on it to operate.

The U.S. is the second largest producer of copper in the world. Still, it's worth noting that all the environmental panic is over less than three percent of the land area in the country. In Arizona, copper mining occupies less that a quarter of one percent of the state's total acreage.

Mining interests and projects are attacked relentlessly with every conceivable argument. A developing copper mine in southeastern Arizona spent $8,000,000 and over two years obtaining 80 of the 82 permits needed to begin operations. A single objection raised by one diehard preservationist was enough to prompt the U.S. Fish and Wildlife Service into action in defense of endangered desert pupfish (*Cyprinodon macularius*) and Gila topminnows (*Poeciliopsis occidentalis*), as well as proposed Bylas springsnails (*Apachecoccus arizonae*), Gila tryonia snails (*Tryonia gilae*) and lowland leopard frogs (*Rana yavapaiensis*)—none of which live near the mine![24] They were simply as a last-ditch effort to shut down a project that would have supplied 200 new jobs to a rural county for at least 17 years.

The Mining Law of 1872 encouraged private individuals to stake and work small mining claims throughout the western unappropriated lands. Latter-day prospectors performed the equivalent of $100 in "assessment work" on these private claims annually to keep them active. Some filed and maintained their claims as a hobby or avocation, some to preserve a piece of American history and some in genuine pursuit of hidden wealth. A provision in the Department of the Interior Appropriations Bill of 1993, however, replaced the $100-assessment-work clause with rental fees that effectively forced 465,000 valid

_____

24-Correspondences between the Greater Gila Biodiversity Project, the U.S. Fish and Wildlife Service and Graham County government are preserved in the author's files.

claimholders to forfeit their holdings. Some could not afford the rent and some did not know about the policy change. In one fell swoop the Interior Department—cheered on by the environmental lobby—reduced the number of claimholders on unappropriated lands by a staggering 61 percent.

It's all about control—*total* control of the land and the resources on it. The anti-mining groups are not above using deceitful tactics to accomplish their end. A myth that has been perpetuated by them is that the Mining Law of 1872 "allows miners to buy federal public land for $5 an acre . . ." Sierra Club, Audubon Society, National Wildlife Federation and others repeat the allegation often.

Dick Swainbank of Fairbanks, Alaska, knows better, but he decided to let the Department of the Interior (DOI) set the record straight. In June of 1994 he wrote to Secretary Babbitt:

Dear Mr. Babbitt,

There has been a great deal of publicity recently on shows such as *Frontline* and *Nightline*, and in the press about the fact that the U.S. Government is selling the rights to mining claims for only $5 per acre. This has been confirmed by statements by Senator Dale Bumpers, and Congressmen Rahall, Vento and Miller, but I was told that you are the person responsible for the land.

Enclosed, please find a cheque (#2480) in the amount of $5 for my purchase of one acre of mining land, preferably in Alaska. I would like an open area on a lake with a view of the mountains. If I have a choice, the claim should have gold, platinum or scandium.

I don't know which agency accepts these payments, so have made the cheque out to you personally, and trust that you can direct it to the correct office.

Dick Swainbank
Fairbanks, Alaska 99708

One month later, Mr. Swainbank received a reply from DOI's Bureau of Land Management office in Washington, DC:

Dear Mr. Swainbank:

Thank you for your letter of June 10, 1994, to Secretary of the Interior Bruce Babbitt, enclosing a check in the amount of $5 for the purchase of one acre of land in Alaska under provisions of the Mining Law of 1872. Secretary Babbitt has asked the Bureau of Land Management's Division of Solid Minerals to respond.

As you know, the patenting of land under the Mining Law of 1872 is not as easy as simply writing a check. The Mining Law of 1872 provides a method of acquisition for Federal land for the sole purpose of mining and producing minerals for the wealth of the Nation. The Mining Law prescribes, among other things, the process of staking claims, the requirements for discovery of valuable mineral deposits, and how to apply for patent to the land involved. For most individuals, the exploration process leading to discovery of a valuable deposit may cost several hundreds of thousands of dollars per claim for drilling and sampling expenses and that expenditure may lead to nothing if no minerals are found or the BLM mineral examiners determine that the requirements of discovery of valuable minerals have not been met.

The Mining Law of 1872 is a complex and controversial issue and is currently undergoing congressional review. The Administration and Secretary Babbitt are committed to the overhaul of Federal policy on mining practices on public lands. However, this complex issue needs to be resolved as fairly and equitably as possible in a way that will be sensitive to the needs of individuals and their livelihoods . . .

We are returning your check and enclosing a brochure which describes the administration of the Mining Law by the BLM. If we can be of further assistance to you, please do not hesitate to contact us.

Paul Politzer
Chief, Division of Solid Minerals

So, a formal letter from the Department of the Interior paints a far different picture of the ease and expense with which miners acquire and "exploit" so-called public lands. And, even here, there is little acknowledgment given for the *necessity* of harvesting minerals and other materials from the earth. The following is a brief list of the sheer quantities of various materials that will be consumed in the lifetime of every baby born in the U.S. during 1991:

(1) 1,238,100 pounds of sand and gravel for homes, schools, offices, factories and roads;

(2) 32,700 pounds of iron for home appliances, kitchen utensils, cars, ships and buildings;

(3) 28,200 pounds of salt for plastic products, detergents, water softeners and foods;

(4) 26,600 pounds of clay for bricks, paper, paint, glass and pottery;

(5) 3,600 pounds of aluminum for beverage cans, house siding, aluminum foil and as an alloy for pipes, steam irons, cookware and aircraft;

(6) 1,500 pounds of copper for electric motors, generators, communications equipment and electrical wiring;

(7)   800 pounds of lead for car batteries, electronic components and solder; and

(8) 750 pounds of zinc for protective coatings on steel and chemical compounds for rubber and paint and as an alloy to make brass.[25]

Mining has played a key role in the building of this most successful nation in the world. It has contributed greatly to the standard of living recognized worldwide as the "American way." Its products are used summarily by those who strive to close off the lands and lock up the resources. Eco-socialists espouse the ridiculous contention that "industrialism itself threatens us," but they are not willing to trade its benefits for a second-class existence in some undeveloped reach of the world.

Every product and substance used by humankind must be either mined from the bowels of the earth or grown from its face. There is no exception.

Another environmental "resource rush" has occurred over America's timberlands. Using endangered species as "surrogates" to enlist the support of lawmakers and judges, the preservationists have locked up millions of acres of forest—both public and *private!* The result has been a "hands-off" approach to forest management that has left

---

25-U.S. Bureau of Mines.

healthy timberland cluttered with dead and dying old-growth, diseased and insect-infested trees, closed canopies and lifeless forest floors—all prime conditions for devastating fire.

It's all about control. It is *not* about protecting species or trees. It is about "land lock"—removing people from the land and preventing them from using it.

Millions of acres of forestland in the Pacific Northwest were taken out of production in 1991 when U.S. District Judge William Dwyer sided with the Sierra Club on the matter of protecting northern spotted owls. It doesn't matter that scientists have proven the "endangered" listing was made on flawed data, or that the species prefers nesting in second-growth timber. It is unimportant that 85,000 industry workers have lost their jobs, or that the price tag for achieving an 82 percent survival rate for the northern spotted owl exceeds $21,000,000,000.[26] It is of no consequence that the Sierra Club, while representing lawsuits of every imaginable description on behalf of the spotted owl, has admitted the bird was chosen as a surrogate to stop logging in the Northwest. Sawmills sit idle and rusting while lumber is imported and prices escalate. Many small timber-dependent communities suffer slow economic starvation as lumbermen retrain to become tour bus drivers and motel clerks.

26-From a 1993 study conducted by Gardner Brown, an economics and environmental studies professor at University of Washington, and Claire Montgomery, and assistant professor of forestry at University of Montana.

No genetic difference has ever been shown between northern spotted owls and other species of spotted owls known to inhabit the western U.S. Still, clear lines of distinction were drawn by the environmental protectionists when using the California spotted owl to stop timber harvest in the northern reaches of that state.

The Mexican spotted owl became the linchpin for locking up nearly 5,000,000 acres of national forest land in Arizona, New Mexico, Colorado and Utah. A preponderance of evidence shows the "threatened" listing for the Mexican spotted owl was seriously tainted by biases and the desperate "need" for a reason to stop timber harvest in the Southwest. It worked. Preservationists pushed for the listing. The U.S. Fish and Wildlife Service granted it in 1993. Sierra Club sued for a "critical habitat" designation and a federal judge ordered the boundaries drawn. On May 30, 1995, the FWS took control of 4,700,000 acres of forestland, almost half of that in Arizona. There was never any consideration of a 1993 U.S. Forest Service report that the Southwest still has as many old-growth trees in its national forests as it did 30 years earlier. No one cared that spotted owl surveys were conducted only on proposed or active timber sale lands. Again, thriving communities with no other industry (Heber, Eagar and Fredonia) turned into ghost towns of the 1990s.

The spotted owl is but a single species used successfully by the eco-groups to restrict the use of public and private lands. Squirrels (the Mt. Graham story), songbirds, snails, tortoises, lizards and rats have all served as effective tools used by eco-saviors against development, resource harvest, recreation and other land uses.

*The Endangered American Dream*_____

Even fish species have gotten into the act. On January 9, 1995, a federal judge in Hawaii signed an order enjoining six national forests in Idaho from allowing any new or ongoing activities to take place on the forest. These forests collectively measure 28,500,000 acres—more than *half the state!* The stroke of a pen in a courtroom 4,000 miles removed from the issue effectively suspended all timber harvest, road construction, mining and grazing activity. Another vast tract of valuable national resource fell into nonproductivity under the guise of protecting two species of Snake River *salmon!*

Environmental activists from the Sierra Club to the Fish and Wildlife Service hooted in victory as workers lost their jobs and economies derailed. It's not about salmon; it's about controlling another 30,000,000 acres of America and the lives dependent upon it. It's about furthering the socialistic agendas of the eco-bureaucrats and anti-capitalist envirogroups. It's about Judy Bari of Earth First!: "*I think if we don't overthrow capitalism, we don't have a chance of saving the world ecologically.*" It is about choking down private property owners to a point of near nonproduction and removing the public from unappropriated lands. Mostly, it's about centralized *control* of an entire country by an enormous envirobureaucracy.

The Tongass National Forest in southeast Alaska is the largest national forest in the nation. It spans 17,000,000 acres of coastline and encompasses 10,000,000 acres of forest. A combination of Native American claims, Wilderness set-asides and other policy changes (including salmon "protection") have left only ten percent of the total land base potentially available to the timber industry. Since

1990, preservationist lawsuits claiming everything from concern for wolves and goshawks to depletion of the forest have stopped most of 23 proposed timber sales. Alaska Pulp Corporation closed mills in Sitka and Wrangell. Over 42 percent of the direct timber employment on the Tongass has disappeared. One-third of the remaining available 10,000,000 acres has been set aside in "habitat conservation areas" for goshawks and wolves although neither has been listed as threatened or endangered.

The onslaught never ends. Eco-groups immediately targeted forests to the east and west of Idaho when six national forests in that state were closed. Preservationists work tirelessly to shut down all resource harvest in Alaska and other states. Every year, U.S. Congresswoman Carolyn Maloney (from Manhattan) introduces her "Northern Rockies Ecosystem Protection Act"—a plan to lock up 16,000,000 acres of wild country as "continuous wilderness" in Montana, Wyoming, Idaho, Washington and Oregon. In 1995, Interior Secretary Bruce Babbitt proposed the Interior Columbia Basin Ecosystem Management Project—a plan to lock up 144,000,000 acres of private, state and federal land in seven western states in the name of "ecosystem management."

Preservationist groups and the enviroagencies have targeted private property as well. The FWS has long managed for threatened and endangered species irrespective of private property boundaries. In June of 1991, a small coalition of landowners and independent timber companies from Oregon filed suit in U.S. District Court, challenging a definition of the word "harm" that included private actions on private land. Government eco-lawyers carried the challenge all the way to the U.S. Supreme Court. In June of 1995, the Court voted five to four that Secretary Babbitt's definition of "harm" should stand, allowing FWS eco-agents to draw a 4,000-acre habitat circle around every spotted owl. This decision (*Babbitt v. Sweet Home Chapter of Communities for a Greater Oregon, et al.*) restricts activity on public *and* private land, and there are *thousands* of *known* nesting pairs of northern spotted owls.

It's all about control.

The preservationists' efforts *create* problems rather than solve them. Unmanaged forests become sick and dangerous. Before the influence of modern man, forests were managed "naturally" with cycles of growth, use and fire. Naturally-occurring densities of wildlife browsed the young forest, keeping ground cover trimmed and controlled. Low-intensity fires swept through quickly, removing noxious plantlife and promoting the start of new seedlings. Old trees died and fell, some consumed by the next fire and some rotting away to provide mulch and wildlife habitat.

Trees have life-spans just like other species of plants and animals. A 1,000-year-old forest does *not* have 1,000-year-old trees. Younger trees grow from the seeds of older trees and the oldest nonproductive trees naturally die. Protecting old-growth forests against all forms of use or management is wasteful and unnatural. Preventing low-intensity fires from cleaning the forest floor makes other forms of management—salvage logging, thinning, controlled burning, grazing—imperative. Otherwise, noxious growth becomes rampant, wildlife is discouraged, the forest cannot breathe, it becomes infested with disease and killing insects, it dies and invites ravaging *high*-intensity fire that kills *everything*—including the soil.

During the summer of 1994, 65,000 wildfires consumed over 4,000,000 acres of western timberland. Tens of *billions* of board feet of valuable lumber were lost. Damage totaled billions of dollars and direct fire suppression exceeded $900,000,000.[27] Intelligent hands-on management of forests once minimized these kinds of statistics. Arizona Senators John McCain and Jon Kyl have both condemned government policies that "suppress proper forest management, reconfiguring the landscape into a virtual tinderbox." Steve Arnos, a fire ecologist at the U.S. Forest Service Intermountain Fire Sciences Laboratory in Missoula, Montana, said in early 1995 that a cumulative area of Ponderosa pine equivalent to the size of Washington state was primed for devastating fire. The problem? Deteriorating health of millions of acres of trees.[28]

Chris Gates of the Alaska Forest Association says, "There is no such thing as an ancient forest. A forest isn't something you can freeze in time. All trees die, only to grow back again. People should have access to a reasonable number of trees to support forest-dependent communities."[29]

27-Statistics provided by Idaho Senator Larry Craig, Chairman of the 1995 Subcommittee on Forests and Public Land Management of the Senate Energy and Natural Resources Committee.

28-*Sunset* magazine, "The Crisis in Our Forests," Jeff Phillips, July 1995, p. 87.

The U.S. Forest Service itself outlines the "History and Objects of Forest Reserves":

> . . . *for the purposes of preserving a perpetual supply of timber for home industries, preventing destruction of the forest cover which regulates the flow of streams, and protecting local residents from unfair competition in the use of the range . . . that the welfare of every community is dependent upon a cheap and plentiful supply of timber . . .*

Traditional timber harvest has *not* depleted the forests of the nation as environmentalists claim. Forest Service documents verify there has been *no* loss of old-growth forests in the Southwest through managed logging since 1960. Since 1940 growth has exceeded harvest in forests of the Pacific Northwest.[30] Additionally, if all the protected old-growth forests in Oregon and Washington (permanent reserves) formed a band across the country, it would occupy a continuous strip two miles wide from ocean to ocean and farther. Northwest reforesting operations average planting six trees for every one taken. Since 1954, logging in the Tongass National Forest has touched only two percent of the land area there.

29-Chris Gates quote and other information on the Tongass National Forest taken partially from *Resource Review*, "Siege Intensifies on Tongass Loggers," April 1995, p. 5.

30-From a report compiled by Roger Sedjo of the nonpartisan consulting group Resources for the Future.

The preservationist community does not care, however, about the original mission of the Forest Service. Neither does it consider the "natural" cycle of forest management nor care about forest health. It cares only about locking up the land and resources. Its agenda is promoted both within the well-funded eco-groups and self-empowered federal bureaucracies. Common sense, logic and good science have been omitted from the discussion.

The same conditions apply to the "resource rush" over rangelands in the West. Eco-groups want cattle removed from all unappropriated lands and the heads of federal regulatory agencies have scraped and bowed in every conceivable manner to accommodate them. In 1995, Jack Ward Thomas—appointed as head of the U.S. Forest Service after leading the effort to "protect" spotted owls in the Pacific Northwest—called for extensive environmental assessments of all 4,500 forest grazing permittees as part of the permit-renewal process. Secretary of the Interior Bruce Babbitt began in 1993 to implement his "Rangeland 94" proposals on all Bureau of Land Management allotments. The plan would claim ranchers' improvements and water rights for the government and replace local grazing advisory boards with "resource advisory councils" loaded heavily with nonlocal ultra-green environmentalists.

Intense environmental media campaigns have gravely misinformed the general urban populace. The average city-dweller believes rangelands are barren and gouged with unchecked erosion because voracious cattle have stripped away all signs of life. Misleading pictures appear in newspapers and on public television. The campaigns are well-financed and effective.

*The Endangered American Dream*_____

Convincing evidence in support of the western ranching industry is seldom seen because the media are more interested in sensational allegations than in anything so mundane as the truth. The "truth" does exist, however, in many forms. First, federal law closely regulates the number of animals and the length of time the animals are allowed to remain on any allotment. Statistics from the Interior Department show " . . . *the range is in better shape than at any point in this century.*"[31] Excellent videos like *The New Rangeland Compact*[32] and *Wetlands Management in Today's Environment*[33] provide powerful arguments in defense of grazing. When exposed to the "truth" in these contexts, even some supporters of Bruce Babbitt's "Rangeland 94" proposals have switched sides in the debate. Perhaps the most definitive book ever written on the vested rights of ranchers on unappropriated lands is *Storm Over Rangelands*, by Wayne Hage.[34]

Conscientious *private* stewardship of both Forest

31-From a June, 1993, Department of the Interior internal memo from staffers Kevin Sweeney and Lucia Wyman to Secretary Babbitt and Bureau of Land Management Directors Jim Baca and Tom Collier.

32-Available at Common Ground, PO Box 147, Payson, AZ 85547, or call (520) 474-6858.

33-Available at Free Enterprise Legal Defense Fund, PO Box 44705, Boise, ID 83711, or call (208) 336-5922.

34-Available at Merrill Press, PO Box 1682, Bellevue, WA 98009, or call (206) 455-5038.

Service- and BLM-managed lands plays a significant role in continually improving conditions for wildlife. Many sources of water exist today across arid stretches of rangeland due solely to the efforts and investments of ranchers. A strong defense for domestic grazing on the range rests in the burgeoning numbers of many kinds of wildlife. A 1990 survey of big game populations on the western rangelands (excluding Alaska) showed a 30 percent increase in the number deer since 1960. In the same period, antelope increased by 112 percent, bighorn sheep by 435 percent, moose by 476 percent, and elk by 782 percent.[35] No one seems to credit the stewardship of ranchers for flourishing densities of wild animals, and large numbers of nondomestic animals are never mentioned when blame is placed for alleged "overgrazing."

Perhaps the best evidence that managed grazing is not the enemy of good conservation can be found today at some copper mines across the West. An experimental project began in 1989 at an Inspiration Copper minesite near Austin, Nevada. Cowboys drove 600 cows onto the steep, barren slopes known as "tailing dams." Project workers tossed hay with grass seed out on the slopes. The cows plowed the hay into the hillsides with their hooves as they grazed. They plowed and fertilized, plowed and fertilized. One worker called it "soil building."

The tailing dams at Austin, Nevada, no longer look like sterile moonscapes. Instead, they yield crops. The

---

35-"State of the Rangelands - 1990," a report from the Department of the Interior, Bureau of Land Management.

project was so successful that it has been copied by other mining companies in other states. Cyprus Climax Metals has virtually ended a severe erosion problem next to a major U.S. highway at Claypool, Arizona. ASARCO at Hayden, Arizona, and Magma Copper at San Manuel, Arizona, have both joined the growing list of successful conservation stories.

Opponents of ranching, mining and timbering are never impressed with success stories such as these, or that resource harvesters are concerned enough about the environment to promote conservation efforts. Neither are they receptive to statistics and studies that do not support their single-sighted agenda. Their only purpose is to control the land, its uses and resources. Their pursuit of total "land lock" is tireless because control of the land also means control of the people.

The nation's productivity, competitiveness and economic health are at stake. Only by harvesting and managing our natural resources wisely can this nation—the strongest and richest nation in the world—continue to function as a leader in the global marketplace. Only by owning and using the land and resources of the nation can its people continue to live and work as "freemen." The alternative is serfdom.

The "Exploited" Species Act

*"I believe there are more instances of the abridgement of
freedom of the people by gradual and silent encroachments
of those in power than by violent and sudden usurpations."*
—James Madison
4th U.S. President

The Endangered Species Act (ESA) has become
the favored tool of preservationists and bureaucrats for
locking up private and public lands. No other vehicle has
achieved as much success in the usurpation of private
property rights and the denial of access to unappropriated
federally-managed lands. Twenty-five ranching families
along the Blue River in remote Greenlee County, Arizona,
know how effective it is.

A serpentine single-track road runs through the Blue
River Canyon. It provides access to and from the outside
world. The road crisscrosses the river as it winds past
picturesque ranches—the homes of working ranch
families—some of them more than 100 years old.

In November of 1994, the Blue flooded, taking the
dirt road with it. Greenlee County officials moved quickly
to authorize emergency repairs. Bill Marks and some other
ranchers began work on the road. The U.S. Army Corps of
Engineers and the U.S. Forest Service ordered them to stop
their work. The U.S. Fish and Wildlife Service (FWS) had

made the decision because the Blue River is "habitat" for the loach minnow, an obscure fish protected by the ESA.

The families in Blue River Canyon found themselves cut off from medical care and mail delivery. They resorted to canned goods in their pantries for food. FWS officials said the road repairs could not be done without "consultations" or the county would face punitive fines as high as $20,000 per day. While holding work at a standstill for weeks, Phoenix FWS Director Sam Spiller contended, "Our concern is that these emergency repairs go forward as fast as possible . . . "

Tim Robart, whose parents moved onto their ranch in 1972, said, "That road is our lifeline . . . They endangered the lives of . . . people ranging in age from three to 85 who live down here."

Marks, a fourth-generation Blue River rancher, said simply, "They're attacking our everyday way of life," and added he was "scared" for his family and livelihood. Marks eventually got permission from FWS to continue work on the road, but only by promising to comply with a long list of conditions.

The long-time residents of Blue River Canyon consider themselves "environmentalists" with a deep interest in taking care of their lands. They know how important the river is to their lives and that it must be preserved. Robart concluded, "I'm a better steward of this land down here . . . and we've got a government agency telling [us] that bugs and birds and rats are more important than people."

The government of Greenlee County would like to build a more permanent road into the canyon—one that will not wash out during future flood events. That project may never occur because FWS has added to its list of concerns potential impacts on habitat for the *Mexican spotted owl!*[36]

In December of 1994 there were over 900 species listed as threatened or endangered. Species were being added to the list every month. Campaigns for listing over 7,000 more species were ongoing in the 50 states. In two decades of ESA enforcement, only six species—four birds, one plant and the gray whale—had been taken off the list as "recovered" species. At the same, *seven* species were removed as "extinct." More than a third of those listed have no plans written to save them. Still, property owners and lands users must comply with management demands that impede property rights and accomplish little else.

Preservationists and envirocrats take credit for successes they have not earned. Recovery of the delisted peregrine falcon and other birds is more logically attributed to the banning of DDT than any so-called "plan" carried out by FWS. The same holds true for the gray whale and international laws passed against hunting it. The ends of DDT and broad-scale whaling came *before* the Endangered Species Act in 1973. There is not one piece of scientific evidence available to show that government officials or environmental activists have contributed anything at all to the recovery of a species. Some of their regulations and actions have accomplished exactly the opposite.

36-Details of the Blue River story appeared as part of a series in *Tribune Newspapers*, "A Battle of Vanishing Species," Chris Coppola, Monday edition, February 20, 1995, p. A7.

In 1994, about 185 Sonoran pronghorn antelope were believed to remain in far southwestern Arizona. Wildlife experts knew little about their range or habits or needs for food and water. Federal biologists captured 22 of them to be fitted with radio-signal collars. Six of the "endangered" animals died after being handled. Similarly, Mt. Graham red squirrels have died of stress in the hands of biologists studying them. Two dozen rare thick-billed parrots "reintroduced" into a pristine canyon in southeastern Arizona froze to death or were eaten by predators. Once thought to be extinct, black-footed ferrets, bred in captivity and released by the hundreds in Wyoming, Montana and South Dakota have become the favored food supply for coyotes.

A bizarre example of the egregious nature of endangered species listing and mitigation enforcement involves a *fly* in southern California. In March of 1992, University of California entomologist Gary Ballmer petitioned the U.S. Fish and Wildlife Service to list the Delhi sands flower-loving fly as endangered. He asked for the action on an "emergency" basis because San Bernardino County had announced plans to expand its medical center. On the *private property* of the county medical facility, Ballmer claimed to have found *eight* Delhi sands flies!

Ballmer's petition—the only petition asking protection for the species—was filled with *non*information:

> . . . *no data are available to indicate actual historic population levels* . . .

> . . . it is presumed that much, if not all, areas of Delhi soils . . . were former habitat . . .
>
> Anecdotal evidence concerning past abundance . .
>
> . . . it is not possible to establish a population density.[37]

FWS moved quickly. The Delhi sands flower-loving fly gained endangered status in September of 1993. FWS agreed to allow expansion of the medical center only after San Bernardino County agreed to move the entire construction project 250 feet north from the original design site and relocate the adjoining parking lot (*away from the flies*), to install and maintain a fence, vegetation barriers and erosion-control structures (*around the flies*) and to police the area regularly for litter and other foreign matter (*undesirable to the flies*).

This ESA enforcement effort cost the residents of San Bernardino County $3,310,199 to mitigate for *eight flies!* Cost per fly: $413,775. Although the life span of Delhi flies is believed to be about one week, the medical center project was delayed for over a year. Based on pre-construction patient numbers, the cost of mitigation equaled

---

37-Excerpts taken from Gary Ballmer's petition for listing, a copy of which is preserved in the author's files.

treatment to 494 inpatients and 23,644 outpatients.[38]

Nothing about the mitigation agreement assures any protection for the species. It was all about eight flies reported to occupy less than two acres of sandy soil in southern California. It was about relegating the significance of human lives to a position somewhere beneath the importance of insects. It was about a lone preservationist imposing his will upon an entire county with the aid of a single-sighted federal bureaucracy, irrespective of economics, human health risk or property rights.

Similar examples of bureaucratic abuse exist across the land. U.S. Fish and Wildlife agents traveled 15 miles onto Richard Smith's Texas ranch, suspecting he might have killed an eagle. They confiscated his pickup truck without evidence of any crime having been committed. They intercepted Smith's 75-year-old father on his way to find out what was happening, forced him out of his truck and took it, too. The elder Smith—a man with chronic heart disease who had suffered five previous heart attacks—was left stranded ten miles from town. No evidence of eagle-killing was ever found and no charges ever filed. It took *nine months* for the Smiths to get their trucks back—even though they were taken by federal agents *trespassing on private land!*

38-From "Impacts of Mitigation for the Endangered Delhi Sands Flower Loving Fly on the San Bernardino County Medical Center," a report prepared by Stephen T. Lilburn, Environmental Co-Chairman of Inland Action Inc., Seventh Street, Building 759, Suite 52, San Bernardino, CA 92408, October 1994, a copy of which is kept in the author's files.

Based on 1995 ESA enforcement standards, the FWS can effectively control any state or portion of it. All the agency needs is the presence of an endangered or threatened species, critical habitat or study area, or a proposal to list a new species. Every state in the union has them. Every state, county and local government is affected by them. Every taxpaying citizen in the nation foots the bill for high mitigation costs and increased prices on commodities.

For perspective (mid-1995), New Mexico residents maneuver their daily lives around the habits and habitats of 27 protected species. They include four mammals: black-footed ferrets, Mexican gray wolves, Mexican long-nosed bats and lesser long-nosed bats. There are eight birds: the American peregrine falcon, the Aplomado falcon, Arctic peregrine falcon, the bald eagle, interior least tern, Mexican spotted owl, southwestern willow flycatcher and the whooping crane. Eleven fish restrict the waterways: the Chihuahua chub, Colorado squawfish, the Gila topminnow, Gila trout, beautiful shiner, loach minnow, Pecos blunt-nosed shiner, Pecos gambusia, the razorback sucker, Rio Grande silvery minnow and spikedace. Other species include the New Mexico ridge-nosed rattlesnake, the Socorro isopod, Alamosa springsnail and the Socorro springsnail.

Some states play host to several times the number of protected species in New Mexico. In California alone, an additional 1,000 species were proposed for listing in 1994. More than half the candidates for listing in all states are invertebrates (slugs, spiders and beetles). Most of these species are never seen by mankind and contribute nothing to the national interest. Still, property rights and traditional land-use rights are stripped away and taxpayers pay more for species protection than for transportation safety, medical research, Social Security or child care.

The Endangered Species Act began as a well-intentioned effort by Congress to improve the chances of survival for some diminishing species. It became flawed and corrupted, however, when radical preservationists began using it as a tool to achieve other goals. During the second decade of its application, the ESA became the most used (and most successful) method for stopping development, restricting resource harvest, arrogating property and controlling people's lives. Rather than providing a program of incentives for property owners and lands users to work *with* wildlife officials, its enforcement policies encouraged enmity toward the law and the species themselves.

Sam Hamilton, an FWS administrator in Georgia who seems to understand the inadequacies of the process, said, "The incentives are wrong here. If I have a rare metal on my property, its value goes up. But if a rare bird occupies the land, its value disappears. We've got to turn it around to make the landowner want to have the bird on his property."[39]

Michael Bean, an ESA expert and chairman of a wildlife program for the Environmental Defense Fund, told a gathering of Fish and Wildlife Service officials, "There is . . . increasing evidence that . . . some private landowners are actively managing their land so as to avoid potential

---

39-*U.S. News and World Report*, "The Best-Laid Plans," Betsy Carpenter, Vol. 115, No. 13, p. 89, October 4, 1993.

endangered species problems . . . by avoiding having endangered species on their property." Bean said, for example, a quarter-century of protection for the red-cockaded woodpecker has resulted only in bringing it nearer to extinction because punitive policies have caused landowners to alter their private habitat areas in ways that discourage woodpecker habitation.[40]

Larry McKinney, Director of Resource Protection for the Texas Parks and Wildlife Department, said, " . . . I am convinced that more habitat for the black-capped vireo, and especially the golden-cheeked warbler, has been lost in those areas of Texas since the listing of these birds than would have been lost without the ESA at all."[41]

Property owners in the Pacific Northwest have begun harvesting private stands of younger timber to avoid regrowth of habitat usable by spotted owls. Listing of the southwestern willow flycatcher as endangered resulted in a slash-and-burn policy by some landowners in Arizona and New Mexico, reducing suitable streamside vegetation. Many examples exist.

40-U.S. Fish and Wildlife Service's Office of Training and Education seminar series, Marymount University, Arlington VA, November 3, 1994.

41-"Reauthorizing the Endangered Species Act - Incentives for Rural Landowners," Larry McKinney, *Building Economic Incentives into the Endangered Species Act*, Hank Fischer, Project Director, and Wendy E. Hudson, Editor, Defenders of Wildlife, Washington, DC, 1993, p. 74.

Michael Bean told his audience of FWS agents, "It's important to recognize that all these actions that landowners are either taking or threatening to take are not the result of malice toward the [species], not the result of malice toward the environment. Rather, they're fairly rational decisions motivated by a desire to avoid potentially significant economic constraints. In short, they're really nothing more than a predictable response to the familiar perverse incentives . . . "

All reasonable argument points to the dismal failure of the ESA. Michael Bean says, " . . . we don't have very much to show for our efforts other than a lot of political headaches." The Act has cost industry, taxpayers and landowners hundreds of *billions* of dollars. It has not saved or recovered a single species. It has served as an avenue for flawed science and nonexistent data to dictate policy and destroy livelihoods and economies. It has become the license for eco-socialists and federal envirocrats to lock up public lands and private property.

Seventy-five percent of listed species in the U.S. depend largely upon private land for their needs. But the battle is no longer about species; it's about control. Federal regulators and environmental activists are not ready to compromise their agenda. Rather than work to preserve species through positive incentives and cooperation with property owners, their only strategy is to tighten the noose of control around their necks.

Case in point? *Babbitt v. Sweet Home.* In 1991, private property owners in and around the small Oregon community sued to free themselves of Interior Secretary Bruce Babbitt's personal interpretation of the word "harm" as contained in the ESA. Babbitt had broadened the definition to include management practices on private lands within two-and-a-half miles of any known owl nest. A federal court found Babbitt's delineation unlawful. Flanked by coveys of fawning preservationists, Babbitt carried his compulsion to control the activities of property owners to the U.S. Supreme Court. Three years after landowners filed the original suit in self-defense of their property rights, they lost. FWS agents drew 4,000-acre circles around hundreds of spotted owl nests. Property owners could not work in their own forests. Land values plummeted. Massive clear-cutting began in yet-unaffected private timberlands. Babbitt's insatiable drive to control the timberlands of the Pacific Northwest ultimately *caused* the loss of thousands of acres of potential habitat for the spotted owl and other wildlife.

During his term as Secretary of the Interior, Bruce Babbitt set up other programs intended to exact new controls and hardships on property owners and lands users. One of them is species "reintroduction."

Babbitt's playing God with the species was apparent in his plan to reintroduce Canadian gray wolves to Yellowstone National Park and neighboring states. Under the plan, FWS agents would trap gray wolves in Canada. The animals would be released into areas of central Idaho, Montana and Wyoming—30 per year for the first five years. By the year 2002, Babbitt wanted to see 300 wolves roaming the region. A few of them, he believed, would come by natural migration southward. Babbitt said Yellowstone "needs the wolf" to restore some natural balance he felt had been lost since eradication of the predators occurred in the 1920s.

Property owners, recreationists and local residents protested Babbitt's plan. The Farm Bureau Federation announced its intent to sue. Ranchers argued that widespread predation would cost them their profits. Wyoming Governor Jim Geringer asked for state-level participation in the project. Babbitt refused, his strongest support coming from envirogroups committed to removing the public from public lands. He committed $7,000,000 in taxpayer money to start his plan. Another $5,000,000 would come later.

Sheep ranchers in 1990 reported losses to coyotes, cougars and other predators exceeding $1,000,000. Ranchers banded together to oppose reintroduction of yet another killer of livestock. Babbitt's enviroagents at the Fish and Wildlife Service addressed their concerns by issuing a list of conditions that would allow a landowner to protect his domestic animals. One, the landowner would have to *see* the wolf " . . . *in the act of killing, wounding or biting livestock.*" Two, the rancher would be allowed to kill only those predators seen attacking livestock if the wolf weighed more than 50 pounds. Third, any livestock wounded or killed must be turned over as evidence to the FWS within 24 hours.

These are conditions applied to *private property owners!* They are costly and impractical since most private rangeland in the region is remote and rugged. Kills are seldom witnessed and almost never found within 24 hours.

On federal grazing lands, ranchers would not be granted permission to kill a marauding predator until six breeding pairs of wolves were established in the area and the FWS had given up on trying to resolve the predation problem themselves.

Heavy livestock losses in Minnesota from 1987 to 1990 forced FWS to recommend that 30 percent of the wolf population there be killed off each year to control the problem. These are the same wolves being set free in Yellowstone. A U.S. Fish and Wildlife study says differing factors between Minnesota and the western states would probably result in *heavier losses* out West! But the plan went on, anyway.

FWS agents released 15 Canadian gray wolves in central Idaho in January 1995, and 14 more in Yellowstone a month later. Within a short time predicted problems were becoming reality. A wolf showed up in Lemhi County, Idaho, 50 miles from its point of release, and killed a newborn calf. Rancher Gene Hussey killed the wolf. Dr. Robert Cope performed necropsies on the calf and wolf. The results were conclusive: the wolf had attacked a live-born calf and was shot to death in the act of eating it.

Meanwhile, a similar "reintroduction" plan was being "studied" in Arizona and New Mexico—this one for the *Mexican* gray wolf. Conditions almost paralleled those of the Yellowstone project. The Blue Wilderness Area is surrounded by livestock grazing allotments. FWS said under the plan 120 wolves would roam the region, killing between 6,000 and 13,000 deer and 1,200 to 1,900 elk. Revenue losses to agriculture (ranching) and recreation (hunting) industries would exceed $2,400,000—more than *$20,000* *per wolf!*[42] Preservationists claim wolves in a "healthy ecosystem" eat only deer, rabbits and other "natural prey." Ranchers know better, as do federal biologists not committed to the preservationist agenda. That is why the Federal Government sponsored the program that eradicated the animals three-fourths of a century ago.

Reintroduction of species does not work. It's a utopian vision that crumbles under practical application. Constant evolution of the ecosystems precludes the idyllic fantasies of envirodreamers. Transplanted razorback suckers become food for high densities of catfish and bass that did not exist in 1900. Black-footed ferrets once outnumbered coyotes. Thick-billed parrots migrated south into Mexico for their own protection. Burgeoning human populations now inhabit the ancient territories of Canadian and Mexican wolves. Instinctive predators do not recognize wilderness boundaries drawn by man.

Pristine pre-Columbian eco-conditions as described by contemporary preservationists never existed. The American West was never a Garden of Eden. The Lewis and Clark Expedition ate most of their animals to keep from starving because game was so scarce. Indian tribes moved their villages when they destroyed the environment around them. The examples are endless in journals and history books written before the "environmental movement" of the 20th century. It was the genius of Western Man that developed the farmlands, harnessed the rivers, replenished

---

42-U.S. Fish and Wildlife Service Draft Environmental Impact Statement, Alternative A—a plan for full wolf introduction.

the rotting old-growth forests, created food and water supplies for wildlife where none had existed before and gave life to desert wasteland. The bounty of the West helped great cities to grow and the nation to become prosperous.

It was accomplished through sheer determination and rawboned effort. It was done because the builders of this new nation could *own* what they settled, produced and created. Their incentive—their driving force—was a thing called "property rights." Unalienable Rights. The Pursuit of Happiness.

The American Dream.

Conservancy or Piracy

"Indeed, one day the historians may put down our era as one where the gradual intrusion of the public upon the private came to deprive Americans of the liberty that was once the envy of the world."

—Fife Symington
Governor of Arizona, 1992

Extreme environmentalism has turned positive incentives for landowners upside-down. Sheer determination and rawboned effort are now met with government regulation. The courts and bureaucrats dole out property rights like some rationed commodity. Sound land and resource management practices bring retribution. Eco-socialists—both inside and outside the government—hold the God-given rights of American freemen in a death grip.

The American Dream might be "endangered," but it's not extinct. Unalienable rights are granted by God—not by government. Interior secretaries and eco-henchmen may impugn them, but they cannot take them away. Property owners and lands users have the letter of the U.S. Constitution and the spirit of the Founding Fathers on their side.

Big Government and the environmental groups, however, have the money to assert their various agendas. They descend on property owners and lands users using many forms of approach (assault)—costly regulations, crippling litigation, direct land acquisition. Government agencies and powerful eco-groups often team up for better results. For example, the Federal Government consumes about 1,000 acres of private land *every day* through tax-funded acquisition. Most of that passes through so-called "nonprofit land trusts." Three of the biggest and most effective such "trusts" are The Nature Conservancy (TNC), The Conservation Fund and the American Farmland Trust.

These "nonprofit" conservation agencies are 501(c)(3) clearinghouses for some very profitable real estate exchanges. TNC, at any given time, owns millions of acres of land across the U.S. It is, in fact, the largest real estate broker in the country. The 1993 operating budget for TNC exceeded $2,700,000 and it gets bigger each year. Assets were approaching $1,000,000,000. TNC also tops the list of wealthy preservationist groups in the world.

TNC is not in the real estate business for humanitarian purposes; it's all about profit. Government agencies consistently pay higher-than-market-value prices for land transferred to them from TNC. In 1989 the U.S. Fish and Wildlife Service paid $4,500,000 for 5,400 acres in Oklahoma appraised at $3,500,000—a slick $1,000,000 profit. The Bureau of Land Management gave TNC $1,400,000 with which to buy 5,529 acres in Oregon. TNC paid the landowner $1,260,000, leaving a profit of $140,000. A 1992 report from the Inspector General of the Department of the Interior showed the National Park Service paid nearly $5,000,000 for 4,200 acres in South Carolina on the strength of an appraisal done *before* the land was devastated by Hurricane Hugo. The same report revealed 64 transactions in which FWS alone paid more than $5,200,000 *over fair market value* for private land acquired through the so-called "nonprofit" land trusts.

There are more than 900 land trusts operating in the U.S. Most of them are not as active, well-known or successful as TNC, but each contributes to the general effort of removing private land from private hands. They play a key role in the mainstream environmental notion that Mother Nature comes first and humankind is nonessential. It is estimated that at least 3,000 so-called "nonprofit" envirogroups (including land trusts) are at work within the U.S., propagating a message of eco-cleansing to all levels of the American foundation—homes, schools, churches, corporate boardrooms, Congress and the White House. Few of them operate with a revenue flow under $1,000,000.[43]

43-*21st Century*, "Who Owns the Environmentalist Movement?" Rogelio A. Maduro and Ralf Schauerhammer, Fall 1992 edition, p.37.

Their work requires money and they have it. How much money? Twelve of the top environmental groups listed 1992 and 1993 budgets as follows:

(1) The Nature Conservancy
    $278,497,634 (1993)

(2) National Wildlife Federation
    $82,816,324 (1993)

(3) World Wildlife Fund
    $60,791,945 (1993)

(4) Greenpeace Fund, Inc. and Greenpeace, Inc.
    $48,777,308 (1993)

(5) Sierra Club
    $41,716,044 (1992)

(6) National Audubon Society
    $40,081,591 (1992)

(7) Natural Resources Defense Council
    $20,496,829 (1993)

(8) Environmental Defense Fund
    $17,394,230 (1993)

(9) The Wilderness Society
    $16,093,764 (1993)

(10) National Parks and Conservation Association
$11,285,639 (1993)

(11) Friends of the Earth
$2,467,775 (1993)

(12) Izaak Walton League of America
$2,074,694 (1992)[44]

The strongest advantage the preservationist groups have over property owners and lands users is their enormous wealth. The 12 richest groups boast cumulative annual budgets exceeding $630,000,000 and fund balances of more than $1,030,000,000. That buys a lot of publicity. A consistent deluge of propaganda to the broadcast and print media begins to take on the color of truth when little information is seen to counter it.

Before the 1990s, landowners' efforts to organize into groups were haphazard at best. The "green" groups, however, range in age from 20 to over 100 years. The preservationists *created* the rules to their game long before property owners and resource harvesters knew there was a game. Large sums from their amassed war chests are dedicated to training their activists, hiring legal and media people and tracking the business of people and organizations (even government agencies) who don't see

---

44-"Getting Rich," A Report by the Center for the Defense of Free Enterprise, 12500 NE Tenth Place, Bellevue, WA 98005, (206) 455-5038, 1994.

eye-to-eye with them.

Some groups (Sierra Club) support their own legal defense funds, set up especially to file lawsuits. As seen in the Mt. Graham Observatory story, costly litigation is a common strategy. Private landowners can seldom compete. Local governments find themselves quickly out-maneuvered. Again, success in the battle often depends on funding to keep it going.

So where do the enviropath organizations get their money? Most of them lie to their memberships. Millions of Americans belong to organizations like Sierra Club, Audubon Society, National Wildlife Federation and the Wilderness Society because they have noble-sounding names. Their massive mailings report unconscionable atrocities committed against the environment by loggers and miners and developers of all sorts. One common lie involves "depleted old-growth forests." A Sierra Club fundraising letter describes the "streams running orange" with pollution near Yellowstone National Park. Another accuses industry of wanting to destroy the Arctic National Wildlife Refuge (ANWR) with widespread oil exploration.

These are only a minute sampling of the lies. In truth, old-growth forests are more abundant today than they've ever been in recorded history. Sierra Club preservationists are fighting the application to *reopen* an old gold mine *outside* Yellowstone which, if permitted, would operate under the most stringent nonpollution standards. The richest oil reserve in America is located under *eight percent* of the 19,000,000-acre Arctic Wildlife Refuge.

A gullible public accepts the lies as truth because the propaganda *looks* believable. They are not shown evidence that the preservationists are "protecting" the old-growth forests to death! They are not shown that mines today are without the towering smokestacks and noxious emissions, that technology has developed environmentally-friendly extracting and smelting processes, that pollutants are contained and recycled. They are not told that oil production in Alaska does not resemble the ancient oil "fields" of Texas, that environment-dependent Inupiat Eskimos will oversee the ANWR Project and create upwards of 500,000 private-sector jobs throughout the United States. They are fooled by the well-crafted rhetoric and scary stories written by highly-paid fund-raising specialists, and they send in their money. *Millions of dollars!* That becomes fodder for stifling production, halting development, impugning individual rights and perpetuating the six-digit salaries of a few in charge of the "movement."

Data available in 1992 showed total revenues of the so-called environmentalist groups exceeding $8,500,000,000—not including the revenues of law firms involved in environmental litigation. This kind of resource base is more than sufficient for the powerful eco-groups to set national policy. No trade organization in the world, for example, comes with as much financial and political clout. Collections from memberships and private contributions account for only about half of the revenues, so where does the rest of the money come from?

Foundation grants. Foundations are the properties of the aristocratic families of America—Ford, Rockefeller, Mellon, MacArthur, Pillsbury and so on. Foundation grants of over $1,000,000 are typical and $20,000,000 to $50,000,000 are not uncommon. The foundations provide funding for specific projects and even seed money for starting new groups with specialized agendas. One such project: Worldwatch Institute, started by Rockefeller money to "alert policymakers and the general public to emerging global trends in the availability and management of resources—both human and natural."[45] By funneling billions of dollars into their chosen projects (exercising their tax-exempt influence), they can choose the political issues addressed by Congress.

Corporate contributions. Corporations are not tax exempt; they do not have to report the way they spend their money. Therefore, it's more difficult to trace their activities. However, an April 1991 newsletter released by Capital Research Center (CRC) in Washington, D.C., said, "The Nature Conservancy's 1990 report reflects contributions of over $1,000,000 from Amoco, over $135,000 from Arco, over $100,000 from BP Exploration and BP Oil, more that $3,700,000 (in real estate) from Chevron, over $10,000 from Conoco and Phillips Petroleum and over $260,000 from Exxon." The CRC newsletter referred to the oil companies as "heavy financial supporters of the very advocacy groups which oppose [their] activities . . . " Conservative estimates place corporate contributions to the environmental movement at more than $200,000,000 per year. Why? The best explanation is: the giant corporations have figured out how to use environmental regulations to break their smaller competitors.

U.S. Government. Yes, funding for the

_____

45-Worldwatch brochure.

environmental movement comes from within government itself. The ranks of the bureaucracies are filled with thousands of preservation-minded bureaucrats— professional environmentalists who feed at the trough of taxpayer funding. The relationship between The Nature Conservancy and the Department of the Interior is one good example. The Environmental Protection Agency (EPA) "hires" eco-groups to conduct costly "studies" on environmental topics ranging from radon gas to global warming. Officially, as of 1992, the Federal Government was giving away more than $3,000,000,000 annually in grants to environmentalists. Unofficially, the amount is inestimable.[46]

The Center for the Defense of Free Enterprise in Bellevue, Washington, uncovered federal records showing The Nature Conservancy received $20,400,000 in taxpayer cash subsidies in 1993. In 1992 World Wildlife Fund got $7,200,000. Defenders of Wildlife received $602,527. National Audubon Society got $505,850 and the Center for Marine Conservation received $680,289 in 1992. These are taxpayer dollars paid directly out of the U.S. Treasury to eco-socialist and preservationist envirogroups in *cash grants*.[47] No strings attached. Not tax breaks. Not loans. GRANTS!

46-Some details on foundation, corporate and government funding are taken from *21st Century* (footnote 43), a copy of which is preserved in the author's files.

47-*The Private Sector*, The Wise Use Memo, Vol. 8, No. 1, Spring 1995, p. 1.

*The Endangered American Dream*_____

Property owners, lands users and resource
harvesters face discouraging odds. Not only is the collective
wealth of their opponents nearly incomprehensible, but their
own war chests are dedicated to complying with
government-imposed environmental *regulation*. In 1994,
the total cost of environmental regulation in the United
States was over $141,000,000,000 (*billion*)![48] It was paid
by industry, which provides jobs, commodities and
economic security; by farmers and ranchers who provide
jobs, food and clothing; by mom-and-pop businesses that
ensure community security and American free enterprise;
and by local and state governments dependent upon the tax
dollars of working citizens. There are *54 federal regulatory
agencies* run by *130,000 agents* costing the American
people *$14,300,000,000!* Just during the George Bush
presidency, federal bureaucracies added 5,000 new
regulations every year. It required 21 feet of library shelf
space to store the 70,000 pages of regulations from a single
year.[49]

The playing field is no longer level. The private
landowner has been stripped of his ability to compete.

"Environmentalism" has become an undercurrent
influencing every facet of American society. It affects
industry and development, gross national product, health,

48-From a report by Thomas Hopkins, Rochester Institute of Technology
Conference on Regulatory Review.

49-*Positions on Property*, Carol LaGrasse, Property Rights Foundation
of America (PRFA), PO Box 75, Stony Creek, NY 12878,
(518) 696-5748.

education, politics and government, social welfare and fundamental civil freedom and human rights. It is a tool used to achieve many objectives. Industry uses it to foil competition. Politicians use it to garner votes and discredit their opponents. Radical eco-groups find it an effective way to advance their political and social philosophies. Bureaucrats employ its broad effects to manipulate the private sector while validating their own self-worth.

Property rights were considered equal to the laws of God by our Founding Fathers. Without the security of private property rights there was no assurance of liberty then, nor is there now. Extreme environmentalism has emerged as the "paganism" capable of consuming and destroying a free America.

Pantheism to Terrorism

"In every civilized society, property rights must be carefully safeguarded; ordinarily and in the great majority of cases, human rights and property rights are fundamentally and in the long run, identical."

—Theodore Roosevelt
26th U.S. President, 1910

In the afternoon of April 15, 1995, Tom Kelly was routinely checking the water tanks on his Tres Lomitas

Ranch near Deming, New Mexico. It was Saturday. The ranch sprawled over 15 sections and it had been a long day.

At a windmill just a mile-and-a-quarter from the ranch headquarters, Kelly found something terribly wrong. Someone had removed a drain fitting at the bottom of a large storage tank used to supply four separate pastures with water. Upon further inspection, Kelly discovered the windmill at the site had been jammed and its sucker-rod broken. Anchor bolts were missing from the legs of the windmill, leaving it standing precariously against any strong gust of wind.

Then Kelly found the carcasses of 13 cows and seven calves slaughtered within two miles of the water tank. The animals had all been shot. They were strung out along a road leading away from the windmill and the ranch headquarters. Subsequent investigation revealed that most of the animals had been shot through their hearts. One pregnant cow was hit with a bullet just above the udders and one calf had been shot in the face. A search for shell casings suggested the brass had been carefully picked up from the area, but one was found. It was a .762 caliber used in Chinese SKS rifles.

The Tres Lomitas Ranch is a 200-head operation on private land supplemented by grazing leases on state-owned and federally-managed allotments. Part of the ranch is included in a Bureau of Land Management "wilderness study area." The dead cattle and damaged water-collection system were all inside the posted study area. The Kellys had held a grazing permit for the area long before it became a potential wilderness and continued to do so at the time of the attack. A BLM designation marker was found on the ground next to the broken windmill.

Two days after his cattle were found dead, Tom Kelly received an envelope postmarked in Las Cruces, New Mexico. It contained material advocating the end of cattle grazing on public lands and a slogan: *Cattle Free in 2003.*

In the weeks prior to the Tres Lomitas incident some newspapers in New Mexico had run letters to their editors from an Albuquerque man who complained about Kelly's cattle roaming around inside a "study" area. In response, the BLM inspected the range and determined that it was *not* overgrazed. Federal agents acknowledged that Kelly's grazing permit was legal and "grandfathered." He had every right to be there.

A disturbing message began appearing on networking computers across the West:

> ### Hunt Cows, not Cougars
> *That's right, shoot cows.*
> *They don't run*
> *They don't bite*
> *They don't charge*
> *They don't maul*
> *They produce only 2% of the beef from 70% of the public lands*
> *A pound of beef requires 2000 gallons of water, a pound of wheat, only 20*
> *There's WAAAY too many of them*
> *Happy hunting.*

Militant radicals of the environmental group Earth First! claimed responsibility for the computer message and for cattle killed elsewhere in the West. Investigators do not feel the attack on Tom Kelly's ranch was a random incident. It was too methodically executed. Proper tools were necessary for taking drain fittings loose and removing bolts from the windmill legs. One rusted bolt had been sawed through. Someone knew how to snap a sucker-rod. Incriminating evidence was picked up and carried away. The loss of livestock alone was estimated at nearly $20,000.[50]

The attack on Tom and Dorothy Kelly's ranch was an assault—an act of terrorism—perpetrated against the fundamental concepts of property rights and land uses in the West. It shows the extreme to which some environmental activists will go to discourage traditional land use. Ranchers and other resource harvesters recognize the frequency and severity of such incidents as a very real threat to life and livelihood.

In late March of 1995 a rancher's bunkhouse, cookhouse and corrals near Fallon, Nevada, burned to the ground. Water facilities on the same ranch incurred heavy damage and BLM signs along the road were destroyed by shotgun blasts. Sheriff's investigators said the arson was done in a way that ensured the buildings would burn swiftly and totally. A week later, someone bombed a U.S. Forest Service office in Carson City.

Attacks such as these occurred with some regularity in Nevada during 1989 and 1990. During the same period,

---

50-Details of the Tom Kelly story were collected from accounts published in *The Courier* newspaper, Hatch, NM, April 20 & 27, 1995, and from personal conversation with Tom Kelly.

the California Cattlemen's office was firebombed and ransacked and a Forest Service office in Washington was destroyed. Earth First! claimed responsibility for several of these events. A number of arrests from the ranks of the militant group followed before its leaders announced in 1991 it was turning to "paperwrenching"—as opposed to "monkeywrenching"—as a more peaceful means of pursuing its ambitions.

The attitude in 1994 became something quite different, however. Earth First! formed its Earth Liberation Front (ELF) and announced it would become the "underground terrorist cell" of the mother group. In March, Earth First!—now acting as public relations agency for ELF—claimed responsibility for $8,000 damage to Allan Wirkkala Logging property in Olympia, Washington, and $10,000 malicious damage to Tobin Logging at nearby Quinalt. A month later the group bragged about a $50,000 arson hit against Bill Burgess Logging at Snoqualmie Pass, Washington.

In May an Internet transmission advocated the killing of cattle. The message came from a representative of Native Forest Network—another front group for Earth First! In July 1994, a Nathrop, Colorado, rancher named Frank Murray lost six head of cattle to gunfire on a national forest grazing allotment. Other Earth First! terrorist activities during 1994 included $480,000 damage to the Tennessee Valley Nuclear Plant; a $350,000 arson fire at Littlejohn Logging Company in Olympia, Washington; malicious destruction of property to at least ten logging companies in Maine; and growing affiliation with foreign insurgent groups (such as Zapatista Army of National

149

Liberation in Mexico).[51]

Earth First! leader Mike Roselle wrote in the January, 1995, edition of the organization's *Journal*:

> "What we want now is nothing short of a revolution. F--k that crap you read in Wild Earth or Confessions of an Eco-Warrior. Monkeywrenching is more than just sabotage, and your goddam right it's revolutionary. This is Jihad, Pal. There are no innocent bystanders, because in these desperate hours, bystanders are not innocent. We'll broaden our theater of conflict."

The call was for increased acts of terrorism. It was effective. Terrorist hits during the first half of 1995 included death threats against prominent individuals in western logging and ranching communities; increased vandalism and bombings at Forest Service headquarters in New Mexico and Nevada; heavy equipment sabotage; dumping a load of manure in the driveway of Hyatt Regency at Vancouver, British Columbia; cattle shot in California and lock-boxes on gates to private and public forestland booby-trapped with explosives and syringe needles. A pack outfitter at Lake Revelstoke, British Columbia, incurred a $30,000 arson fire and a letter followed to the Revelstoke *Times Review*:

51-*Report on Terrorism*, Barry Clausen (investigator), North American Research, PO Box 65296, Port Ludlow, WA 98365, (360) 437-0453.

"Anyone doing business in the massacre of wild animals, as well as those in related industries, are 'fair game.' We will not rest until the war against Earth ceases."[52]

Earth First! is not the only dangerous environmental group. There are many, including Greenpeace, Pacific Crest Biodiversity Project, Animal Liberation Front, Hunt Saboteurs, Earth Night Action Group, Farm Freedom Fighters and others lesser known. They engage in terrorist acts against ranchers and miners, trailbikers and backpackers, medical research facilities and zoos, rodeos and golf courses. They pour sugar into the fuel tanks and crankcases of road-building equipment. They bury spikes in hiking and biking trails to cause damage and injury. Steel and ceramic spikes driven into trees have resulted in the maiming and deaths of loggers and millworkers. Believing anything "unnatural" is harmful to the environment, the militant activists think of themselves as eco-guerrillas fighting a war. Getting arrested for sabotaging a nuclear generating station is like receiving a badge of honor or courage.

Some militant leaders have written books promoting their dangerous agenda. The bible of eco-saboteurs is *Ecodefense: A Field Guide to Monkeywrenching*, edited by Dave Foreman (founder of Earth First!) and Bill Haywood. The book (two editions) is a step-by-step instruction manual

---

52-All the incidents of terrorism mentioned generally in this section are detailed in *Report on Terrorism* (footnote 51).

on how to disable heavy equipment, cut down billboards, spike trees and roads and how to set booby traps against innocent people in pursuit of their livelihoods and recreation. The clear intent of the instructions is to disrupt and damage, maim and kill.

Another published diatribe against property owners, lands users and resource harvesters is *A Declaration of War: Killing People to Save Animals and the Environment*, by Screaming Wolf. Published in 1991 by Patrick Henry Press, the book advocates the end of human society and surrender of the earth to the creatures that are "the true inhabitants of the planet." It encourages its readers to cheat and steal, lie and plunder, disable, threaten and physically harm those in the way of the stated agenda. It demands that so-called "liberators" destroy roads, burn research facilities, kill researchers and disrupt the "machinery of society."

The so-called "Unabomber"—a group or individual believed responsible for some 16 terrorist incidents between 1968 and 1995, including at least three deaths—has written letters linking "his" eco-Nazi agenda to such publications as *Earth First! Journal* and *Wild Earth*, as well as *A Declaration of War: Killing People to Save Animals and the Environment.* In 1990, *Earth First! Journal* published a list of 12 corporations dubbed "Eco-f--ker Hit List." Three of the twelve became targets of the Unabomber within the next five years.

While the threat of enviroterrorism is very real, not all environmentalists are terrorists. There are three fundamental groups of eco-preservationists. Radical far-left organizations (such as Earth First! and other militant extremists) are by far the most dangerous. They know no compromise. They shun accepted legal procedures and they hate everybody else—especially other environmental groups that do not subscribe to their standards. They find fulfillment in causing their enemies financial and physical harm. Their objectives are unreachable, so they color themselves as martyrs for their cause.

The middle road of the environmental movement is occupied by "interventionists." These are the Sierra Clubs and Audubon Societies with the means and determination to block any and all forms of progress and development with litigation. The enemies of the interventionists are not people and corporations so much as the activities required for them to succeed (survive). Logging and mining, for instance, require the taking of resources from the earth. Interventionists believe timber and minerals should not be disturbed from their natural state and they have perfected legal roadblocks to prevent their harvest. Other uses of the earth (ranching, farming, recreation) are equally undesirable. The interventionists are very hypocritical, however, because they eat food, wear clothing, live in houses, drive automobiles, use computers and produce reams of paper documents—all of which require resources from the earth.

Eco-socialists (Wilderness Society, Greenpeace) make up the third fundamental group. Their agenda is the destruction of capitalism. Unlike the Sierra Club, their enemies *are* the corporations, the ranchers and farmers, entrepreneurs and businesspeople who depend on a "bottom line" to survive. Eco-socialists abhor private property rights and the constitutional protection of civil liberties and freedom (such as the right to keep and bear arms) because socialism depends on subservience for its own existence.

The general population cannot be free to do as it pleases; it must be dependent on the system. In the "perfect" socialistic world, rich people would be poorer and poor people richer, strong nations weaker, weak nations stronger, and all the resources of the world would be rationed equally to all the consumers. Of course, enormous caches of wealth and resources would be held in reserve for the Socialist government leadership. It's a formula that has failed hundreds of times around the world; not one experiment in socialism has ever succeeded.

Still, government bureaucrats embrace the ideology. Why? Because it puts them in positions of power. The Interior Department of the U.S. Government has burgeoned with agencies and agents bent on controlling all the land, resources and property owners in America. Under the leadership of Secretary Bruce Babbitt after 1992, policies were carried out that stripped away legal rights to mining claims, water and multiple uses of unappropriated lands across the West. In an effort to take control of *private* property from coast to coast and border to border, Babbitt devised the National Biological Survey (NBS) in 1993.

The NBS was Babbitt's plan to map all the species of the nation, leaving no spot of earth unchecked. Private property rights would cease to exist as environmental volunteers fanned out to chart the species. The program received funding in a 1993 Interior appropriations bill, but the agency itself was never authorized by Congress. Instead, Babbitt set up the project "administratively," renaming it Life Sciences Research and placing it within the National Geological Survey. In 1995, funding from the so-called "research" project went to state wildlife management agencies for work on charting the species. Of course, with the *Babbitt v. Sweet Home* Supreme Court decision in June of 1995, any endangered or otherwise "sensitive" species found on private property could be managed by the Interior Department as if it were on public land.

This is why the "eco-socialist" groups do not sue the Federal Government over environmental issues like the "interventionist" groups do. Instead, their members are often hired to work as government agents. George Frampton, one-time president of Wilderness Society, became a top-level assistant to Bruce Babbitt. Jack Ward Thomas, champion of northern spotted owls, was appointed to head the U.S. Forest Service. The ranks of these agencies are filled with "greens." Anti-capitalists and envirocrats are on the same mission—to dismantle the concept of free enterprise in America. The interventionists, on the other hand, *do* sue the regulatory agencies over timber sales, critical habitat designations for species, wild and scenic rivers, permitting of cattle grazing and mining operations and other projects (i.e., telescopes on Mt. Graham).

And there's a fourth category of "environmentalist" that's really not a *category*; it's more like a cult—and close cousin to Earth First!like radicals. To them, environmentalism is a religion. It has many names. Webster's defines "pantheism" as: *the doctrine that all forces, manifestations, etc. of the universe are God.* Other elusively descriptive labels for enviroworship include animism, noeticism, organicism, mysticism and transcendentalism. They all mean the same thing—that humans do not have any special status over other species or objects in the universe.

155

In a book entitled *The Earth Religion*, Dr. Sydney Singer describes the ideology:

> "**God is nature.** God is the stream, the rock, the tree, the flower, the squirrel being, the worm being, the eagle being, and the minnow being. God is the land the beings walk on, the air they breathe and fly through, the water they drink and swim in. God is the Earth, the moon, and the stars. God is the clouds, the rain, and the snow. God is the relationship between all these various energies and forms of matter. **God is the flow of all that is.**"

Singer calls the tendency of humans to think of themselves as the center of the world "anthropocentrism." He says humanity must adopt a doctrine of "naturocentrism" instead because human beings "are no more important than snail beings, squirrel beings, bee beings and cow beings." A belief in naturocentrism rejects the notion that humans should see and use nature as a "natural resource." Therefore, such activities as timber harvesting, mining and ranching, farming, fishing, hunting, gardening, or *living* as humans typically do, are all transgressions against the god called Nature.

Singer describes a series of "animal rituals" designed to bring humans greater sensitivity toward their god (animals and plants). One of them is the Small Animal Ritual:

> "Look in your backyard, the forest, or even in your home for an insect, such as an ant, beetle, fly,

caterpillar, etcetera. Observe the little being, including his or her eating, grooming, walking, and resting behaviors. If it would not disturb the creature, let him or her walk on your hands and arms. What does it feel like? Can you smell the creature? How does the insect respond to the hairy and smooth parts of your skin? After you have gotten to know this being for at least fifteen minutes, place the insect back where you found him or her."

Others are called the Night Walk Ritual, Primal Music Ritual and the Ritual of Grooming, which requires massaging sesame seeds into people's scalps, then picking them out and eating them. Then, of course, there's the Grazing Ritual:

"Kneel down in a field of grass. If you wear eye glasses, take them off. Now bend down with your face touching the blades of grass. Move your face from side to side, feeling the texture, stiffness, moisture, and coolness of the grass. Smell the aroma of the ground. With your tongue, touch several blades. Without using your hands, bite off some grass to chew. What does it taste like? Is it bitter, sweet, or some other flavor? Now roll in the grass and feel it underneath your body."

Most farmers, ranchers, recreationists, property owners and resource harvesters are in tune with the environment around them. They appreciate the smell of soil and wet leaves. They know and love animals. They feel a commonness with nature that comes from living with it, depending on it, protecting it from the ravages of over-population, sickness, disease and fire, but not from contrived rituals. Dr. Singers calls *The Earth Religion* the "first religion for atheists." He and his wife Tanja co-founded a group called A.B.A.C.E. Visions (acronym: All Beings Are Created Equal). His book was self-published in 1991 by A.B.A.C.E. Publications, 10175 Joerschke Drive #215, Grass Valley, California 95945—the same address given for Patrick Henry Press on the copyright page of *A Declaration of War: Killing People to Save Animals and the Environment*, by Screaming Wolf.

Alston Chase, scholar and author of *Playing God in Yellowstone*, refers to the perceived equality of all beings in an ecosystem as "biocentrism." He dismisses the idea as bogus because ecosystems are "mathematical tools" used by scientists to analyze "energy feedback loops." They cannot be drawn on maps. No one can define one. And, says Chase, there is no evidence that an ecosystem left undisturbed would ever reach some kind of equilibrium. It's all a ploy to take control of more real estate—*lots* more.

Example? The Wildlands Project. Conceived by Dave Foreman, founder of Earth First! Endorsed by Bill Clinton, Al Gore, Bruce Babbitt and many others. Acted upon at the United Nations Earth Summit in Rio de Janeiro in 1992. Signed as a treaty by 150 nations. Shunned by President Bush. Signed by Clinton. As of late 1995, still awaiting ratification by the U.S. Senate. Objective: to remove roads, dams, powerlines, cities, towns and all other man-caused disturbances from about half of the land area of the United States. People would be allowed to inhabit low-impact areas and "human buffer zones" within the ecosystems. Wolves and grizzlies, woodpeckers and snails would take precedence. The Convention on Biological Diversity is working from Wildlands maps already drawn by Dave Foreman and other radical preservationists.[53]

The road ahead for property owners and lands users is not an easy one. The battle for God-given, constitutionally-protected "unalienable" rights will not be easily won. Adversaries are many, their agendas diverse. They use their great wealth, propaganda and lies, even criminal activity, to effective advantage. They buy the support of elected government officials. They get themselves elected to office. They manipulate the legal system and befriend the media. They indoctrinate impressionable young activists. They pump their curricula into the public education system, turning young children against their own parents who own property and work the land.

The best weapons for preserving the right to freely own and use property are knowledge and truth. The preservationists who work to destroy property rights can only fight truth with lies, knowledge with misinformation.

53-"At least half of the land area of the 48 conterminous states should be encompassed in core reserves and inner corridor zones within the next few decades." *Wild Earth*, "The Wildlands Project," December, 1992. *Science*, "The High Cost of Biodiversity," June, 1993, Vol. 260, pp. 1868-1871. The United Nations' *Global Biodiversity Assessment*, Chapter 10.4.2.2.3. *Convention on Biological Diversity*, Article 8a-f.

When challenged, their arguments do not hold up well. It's difficult to *document* fiction.

The Founding Fathers believed the rights of property were the backbone of a free republican society. Their convictions inspired a unique experiment in government. That experiment resulted in development of the freest, richest and strongest nation in the history of the world. The Founding Fathers were not "visionaries" (defined by Webster's as those " . . . *whose ideas, etc. are impractical.*"); they were "prophets" of freedom. Believing God is good, God is truth, God is right, the Founders strived to protect the right to property equally with the right to life. Most of the effort to dilute property rights is rooted in godlessness.

The rights of property owners and lands users should be of paramount importance to everyone because their loss will affect all of society. Consumer goods will cost much more. Demand will far exceed supply. Society as a whole will suckle the breast of government subsidization until it is dry. Crime will become the vanguard of survival. Dependence on government will grow. Godless socialism will thrive. Anarchy and tyranny will prevail. Freedom will cease to exist.

Defenders of property rights must join forces. Remember, many tactics of your opponents can be effective aids to your own campaign. Get involved in politics. Organize a loud and strong voice. Lobby—*persistently!* Never let elected lawmakers forget your presence or position. Don't allow the voice of the opposition to drown you out. The power of the individual vote still belongs to the people. Run for office. Government is not the enemy when used to further your own agenda; it has worked well for the opposition.

Use the courts and media. Don't lie. Be prepared to *document* the truth. Join property rights groups and coalitions; they provide valuable information and an element of strength in their numbers. Never allow your thirst for information to be fully quenched. Share your knowledge with civic groups, your church, local governments, letters to the editor. Examine your local school curriculum and, if necessary, challenge your local elected school board (in numbers) to change it.

A loud united voice will echo many times and deliver a stronger message than many quiet ones. Civil disorder is ineffective. Violence is counterproductive (not to mention asinine). Complacency is a luxury no one can afford. The will of the people must be asserted. If "freedom"—as defined in the Declaration of Independence and recognized by the U.S. Constitution—is to survive in America, then "defeat" cannot be a part of the vernacular. Failure cannot be an option.

Only free Americans can preserve American freedom.

Fighting Back

The Western States Coalition

"We can safely rely on the disposition of the state legislatures to erect barriers against the encroachment of the national authority."
—James Madison
4th U.S. President

The Western States Coalition (WSC) was founded in 1993 to represent the interests of state and local governments dealing with burdensome federal over-regulation. Some elected officials in Utah, Arizona and other western states agreed that a united front against increasing federal usurpation was the best way to stand up for constituents' rights. By early 1996, representatives from nearly half the states had attended at least one of five "summits" held consecutively in Denver, Phoenix, Salt Lake City, Albuquerque and Portland. Seminars, workshops and networking between hundreds of delegates resulted in a cooperative effort involving thousands of constituents. Membership increased to more than 3,000 county commissioners, state legislators, mayors, natural resource industries, recreational groups, grassroots organizations and municipalities.

Since the first summit in Denver, WSC has been instrumental (and successful) in lobbying for congressional action on unfunded mandates. Many new WSC members were elected to state and local offices in November of 1994. The coalition fought successfully for forest legislation, helped to establish "constitutional defense councils" in several western states and played a key role in reducing funding for the intrusive National Biological Service in 1995.

The business of WSC is rooted deeply in the words and actions of America's Founding Fathers. Coalition members believe the best place for political decision-making is at the level of government closest to the people affected—federal, state, county, municipal. One size does not necessarily fit all. They advocate intelligent use and management of natural resources and environmental policies that balance the scale between species protection, recreational access and healthy regional economies. Property rights are paramount.

WSC has adopted official positions on 12 specific issues:

(1) **Endangered Species**

The law must balance human and economic needs with the needs of plants and animals. The Endangered Species Act of 1973 may have started as a good law, but it became terribly flawed in its interpretation and application. It became a Pandora's box, putting thousands out of work, stopping scientific and commercial progress, closing schools, destroying property values, creating ghost towns and threatening farming, ranching and resource-related industry across the nation. The law must be applied with voluntary incentive-based programs that create a desire in America's landowners to *attract* sensitive species to their properties.

(2) **Private Property**
    Private property must be protected from excessive bureaucratic regulation. Private property rights are as fundamental as the rights to life, liberty and the freedom of speech and religion. The right to property does not mean the right to pollute or cause harm to a neighbor's property; state pollution, zoning and nuisance laws already prevent landowners from abusing the rights of their property. Property rights and environmental protection can coexist, but unreasonable federal regulation reduces property values, creates disincentives to protect species, destroys heritage and cultural values and disproportionately increases costs. States should authorize private property ombudsmen to assist citizens with property rights problems, and when private property is taken for public use, the public should pay for it.

(3) **States' Rights**
    The Founding Fathers characterized people and the states as the source of political power. Therefore, political and regulatory decisions must be made at the level of government closest to the people affected. Only with state and local governments responding to the needs of local constituents and using financial resources efficiently to meet those needs, will political policy reflect accurate environmental, cultural, economic and community

sensitivities. There must be a healthy balance between state and federal governments to establish responsible public policy in issue areas, including, but not limited to, endangered species, forestry, mining, rangeland management, water rights, federally administered lands, access to unappropriated lands, environmental quality, federal mandates, the economy, transportation, education and human services. A delineation between the states and Federal Government provides the best approach for formulating and executing policy.

(4) County Movement

Local governments must have a strong voice in decisions that affect their areas. The U.S. Constitution was crafted with the intent that governmental power be distributed and implemented at a level as close to the people as possible. Local government powers and purposes must be reaffirmed. Counties must be recognized as equal partners in the governing process. Federal laws such as the Federal Land Policy and Management Act (FLPMA) and the National Environmental Policy Act (NEPA) require coordination in planning processes between county and federal agencies. Therefore, higher levels of government should not enact programs or restrict revenue streams that cause burdens on local government without local government agreement. State governments must be recognized as the governing entities within state boundaries and counties within county boundaries. Counties should oppose any planning system than fails to recognize county authority and jurisdiction. Counties should develop specific county land use plans as recognized under federal laws such as NEPA and FLPMA.

(5) **National Environmental Policy Act (NEPA)**

Since its inception in 1969, NEPA has been the object of political grappling. The Act is a procedural law and a law of disclosure. The heart of the Act requires an Environmental Impact Statement (EIS) or Environmental Assessment (EA) for any federal action that might impact the environment. On the other hand, agencies must disclose to decision-makers and the public what society stands to gain or lose with each decision. While NEPA "encourages productive and enjoyable harmony between man and his environment," federal agencies have focused on the environment to the exclusion of humankind. Federal regulators use NEPA to stall development projects, resource harvest and grazing permits. There is nothing in the Act that requires an EIS for a grazing lease or permit. Permit rights are private property, and the Federal Government must honor these leases and permits. To do otherwise is a violation of the law. Animal Damage Control (ADC) has existed on federally managed lands since 70 years *prior* to the enactment of NEPA. Therefore, the Act should not affect ADC. Federal agencies must consult, coordinate and cooperate with state and local officials when conducting EISs *before* the scoping process begins. Economic impacts must also be weighed. The Supreme Court has ruled that federal agencies are " *not constrained by NEPA from deciding that other values outweigh the environmental costs.*" Such balance must be achieved.

(6) **Federally Administered Lands**

The Federal Government controls one-third of all the land in the U.S.—most of that in the West. Almost 88 percent of Nevada, for instance, is controlled by federal government. Federal agencies make decisions and set policies for these lands that otherwise would be under state or local domain. The economies of western states are entirely dependent upon access to the vast federal land holdings. All traditional uses of the lands from recreation to prudent resource harvest must be preserved. Emphasis must be placed on multiple use. National Park expansion and species reintroduction must cease. States manage their lands more efficiently and cost effectively than the federal agencies, therefore, all Bureau of Land Management (BLM) lands should be turned back to the states. The shift would save $559,150,000 per year. The states would achieve a greater profit and U.S. taxpayers would be relieved of a heavy layer of inefficient bureaucracy. State lands are traditionally better maintained and regulated than so-called "federal" lands, and individuals who live in a region should be involved in decisions on how to manage and protect the resources around them.

(7) **Wilderness**

Wilderness lands are defined and regulated by the Wilderness Act of 1964. States are willing to cooperate with the Federal Government in designating and protecting wilderness areas. However, the government must recognize that wilderness designations permanently prohibit states from certain economic activities that affect communities and people. Further, such designations depreciate the values of state inholdings and adjacent state lands, reducing an important revenue source. Congress must pass fair and equitable state wilderness legislation that recognizes only the legal definition of wilderness lands in the 1964 Act. All lands not designated as wilderness should be released from Wilderness Study Area status, and the Bureau of Land Management should be prohibited from making further "study area" designations without express authorization from Congress and state legislatures. Wilderness designations must not result in the loss of state or private lands or increase federal land ownership. Water rights must not be locked up by wilderness designations. Because much municipal, industrial and agricultural water comes from so-called "public" lands, access for the management and maintenance of reservoirs, pipelines and other facilities on watershed lands must be reserved for state and private entities. Historic customs and cultures must be preserved. States must retain the ability to develop land resources for economic stability. Local governments and communities must be included from the beginning in state and national wilderness proposals.

(8) Water Rights

Water rights must be kept sovereign to the individual states. In recent years federal changes in water policy without congressional review have seriously affected century-old water laws, hindering the ability of private citizens, local entities and the states to manage and develop water supplies. Water sources in the arid West are often created by the users of the land— ranchers, miners, municipalities. Ranchers and others on western lands pay for the development of water sources that benefit man, cattle, industry and wildlife. The Federal Government must not be allowed to dictate water policy to the states. National water policy cannot recognize the unique laws, policies, characteristics and applications of individual states. The sovereignty of western water rights must be protected, securing the Bureau of Land Management lands and bringing them under state supervision and management. Congress must recognize the negative effects of Wild and Scenic River designations on rural western communities. Rangeland reform proposals must recognize and preserve the states' traditional primacy in water law. Any effort by the Federal Government to take control of water in wilderness areas is unacceptable and threatens the survival of rural communities and the private lands they serve.

(9) **Rights-of-Way**
Existing rights-of-way across federally managed lands must be preserved. Congress granted rights-of-way across federal lands for the purpose of constructing highways in 1866. The law (RS 2477) allows the word "highway" to substitute for a long list of passageway terminology—road, trail, street, pedestrian trail, horse trail, livestock trail, dog sled trail, jeep trail, mine-to-market road, alley, path, tunnel, bridge, irrigation canal, mail route, ditch, pipeline and others. The provision was repealed in 1976. However, highways, roads and other traditional access routes established *before* that date are grandfathered as protected rights-of-way. Congress must not be allowed to narrow the parameters and restrict the context of "highways." Existing rights-of-way across federal lands are

critically important to states and their residents. States must control these important "highways." The Federal Government must formally recognize all RS 2477 "highways" in order to preserve access for hunting and fishing, mineral development, wildlife management, water maintenance, hobbies and recreation, livestock and timber management, access to private inholding, public safety, trust land management and commerce. States must have access through federally managed lands and maintain local use of these "highways" for public and private purposes, including management of state school-trust lands and exercising rights of ownership in private property.

(10) **Forestry**
    The U.S. contains some of the most valuable, diverse and productive forests in the world. Timber harvest provides clear land for agriculture and development, forest products for a growing nation and more than 1,600,000 direct jobs. Wildfire consumed 4,000,000 acres of forestland in 1994. Forest policy must allow active management of national forestlands for improved health of ecosystems, enhanced social and economic well-being and superior conditions for wildlife conservation. Responsible resource consumption promotes balance between harvest and renewal; nonmanagement results in devastation by insects, disease and fire. Forest policies must recognize local participation in solution-oriented decision-making. The rights of private owners of timberland must be protected and preserved. Salvage-harvest of dead and dying trees must be allowed to reduce the threat of fire, control insect infestation and generally improve forest health.

(11) Mining

Mining is important to the nation and must be encouraged. Any reform of the General Mining Law of the United States should strive to maintain a strong domestic mining industry. Sound environmental stewardship must be practiced through compliance with federal and state laws and standards. A healthy mining industry provides materials for the production of all consumer products, research, technology and defense and substantial revenues for the national and local economies. Net royalties paid to the government must be reasonable and not punitive, based on fair market value. States must maintain primacy in environmental oversight. Regulations must include statutory bonding for mining projects and a rigorous enforcement policy for violators. A significant portion of royalty receipts must be earmarked for an Abandoned Mine state-run cleanup program. The interests and rights of small miners and prospectors must be protected.

(12) Grazing/Rangeland Management

The Federal Government has placed many constraints on western livestock grazers with permits and leases on federally managed lands. The Taylor Grazing Act of 1934 and other federal laws provide for the use of federal lands for managed livestock grazing. The permits and leases are taxed as property. Therefore, the permits and leases must be protected as private property. Rangeland policy must reflect a balance between socioeconomic and environmental issues. Any decision on grazing issues and rangeland reform must be based on the sound science of sustainability and viability, not ideology. States and local residents must participate in any rangeland plan affecting local economies, customs and cultures. Federal grazing fees must remain reasonable, based on fair market value, rather than punitive or exacted as a tool to remove ranching operations from so-called "public" lands. Federally managed lands not designated for enumerated constitutional purposes should be divested to the states and/or counties in which they are located. Onerous regulations contained in the Endangered Species Act, the Clean Water Act, the Clean Air Act, the National Environmental Policy Act, etc., must not be used as weapons against viable stewards of the land managing legitimate grazing operations.[54]

The Western States Coalition is not just for western states. Membership and participation are encouraged for elected officials from municipal and county governments across the nation. Resource harvesters in Maine are as welcome as those in Montana. Steel mills burdened with over-regulation in Pennsylvania can benefit the same as mining companies in Nevada. Wheat producers in Nebraska share complaints about environmental overkill similar to those of cotton growers in Texas. Endangered species regulations affect timber cutting in South Carolina just as they do in Alaska. Land acquisition by the Federal Government threatens private property in Manassas, Virginia, just as it does in, Moab, Utah. Wetlands

---

54-Position statements from Western States Coalition Summit IV, Albuquerque, NM, July 12-15, 1995, are preserved in the author's files.

regulations impugn landowners' rights from Florida to California. The effects of wildfire on Long Island are as devastating as they are in Yellowstone. The prices of beef, lumber and automobiles in Manhattan are driven higher by increasing federal intrusion into resource industries located in Wyoming, Oregon and Arizona.

Voters and taxpayers in communities large or small should ask their elected councils if they are members in the Western States Coalition. If not, ask if they are familiar with WSC doctrines and goals. Local residents should petition county governments to become active in this important body. Private employers in industry and commercial production in the East are as key to the ongoing success of America as mining and ranching in the West. Employees should encourage them to join and participate.

Remember, the loudest voice is often the only one heard. WSC has become a strong lobby in Washington for the rights of individual property owners and wage earners across America. Additional information on WSC membership and participation may be obtained by contacting these leading members:

Met Johnson, co-founder: 801/586-4239 (Utah)
Gail Phillips, co-chair: 907/465-3720 (Alaska)
Mark Killian, co-chair: 602/542-5729 (Arizona)
Mel Brown, co-chair: 801/538-1930 (Utah)
Carolyn Paseneaux, advisor: 307/237-1476 (Wyoming)
Caren Cowan Bremer, coordinator: 505/257-6788 (NM)

Nye County and Other Movements

"The reason why men enter into society is the preservation of their property."

—John Locke
English philosopher, 1690

A major property rights problem in the West is related to the disproportionate amount of land held and controlled by the Federal Government. For example, nearly 88 percent of Nevada is "owned" by government. That leaves 12 percent of the state to generate local tax revenues, sustain municipal economies and provide livelihoods for the entire population. In some counties across the West, as little as *two percent* of the land is privately owned. Consequently, laws were enacted more than a century ago that encouraged the use of so-called "public" land for private purposes—ranching, logging, prospecting, mining—as a way of supplementing livelihoods and encouraging colonization of the West. These activities also provided the much-needed raw materials for building cities and infrastructure, advancing technology, defending the nation and feeding the national treasury.

Only after World War II was the convoluted

ideology spawned that Americans can live without a continuing supply of American resources. The new "environmentalism" became such a popular revolution—especially after a bloody and unpopular Vietnam—that Congress quickly signed on, passing warm and fuzzy conservation legislation aimed at protecting species and environmental conditions. In most cases there was no debate over negative impacts on the human species. No one dreamed that endangered species enforcement would evolve to sawmills shutting down in deference to owls or farms lying fallow where lizards or rats might be present. No one fathomed that clean water protection would prevent the restabilization of flood-torn streambanks and the loss of millions of private acres to erosion. No one foresaw that federal agencies would turn into taxpayer-funded preservationist organizations bent on suspending multiple uses of unappropriated lands and locking up millions of acres in wildlife and ecosystem preserves.

Early in the final decade of the 20th century, some western property owners and lands users realized how desperate their situation had become. They began an all-out battle for their lives. Catron County, New Mexico, set up an effective Comprehensive Land Use Plan[55]—based on federal laws that *require* federal agencies to participate in "joint action" with county governments. Although local counties

---

55-Complete details and instructions appear in *Surviving the Second Civil War* (footnote 7), pp. 161-164. Copies of the actual documents may be purchased from: Catron County Administrator, Catron County Government, Reserve, NM 87830. (505) 533-6423.

have legal standing to assert themselves to federal agencies in decision-making processes, no federal agency is going to *invite* the participation. It must be done according to the law (in this case, NEPA). The "County Land Use Plan" has become the war shield for hundreds of counties from Missouri to Alaska, but thousands more have either failed to initiate the arduous procedure for adopting one or do not know the option exists.

Every county in the nation should have a Comprehensive Land Use Plan. It is not fail-safe. However, having an adopted guideline for legitimate participation in federal decisions affecting local counties is far better than learning too late what the bureaucrats have decided by themselves. A Land Use Plan is a federally-recognized "license" to join the table.[56]

Some counties have begun action to take over the administration of federally managed lands. Otero County, New Mexico, ranchers filed suit in 1995 against Interior Secretary Bruce Babbitt and others, demanding to pay their annual public land grazing fees directly to Otero County. Fees are typically paid to the U.S. Forest Service and Bureau of Land Management. Otero County Attorney John Howard represented the local ranchers' group, calling the action "the first round." He added, "This nightmare is not going away. The litigation will continue until the Federal Government turns back the land to the states and the people."

56-More information: Coalition of Arizona/New Mexico Counties, PO Box 125, Glenwood, NM 88039-0125. (505) 539-2709.

In 1993, Nye County, Nevada, challenged the Federal Government over the "ownership" of all public lands in the state. Nye County Commissioner Dick Carver—asserting the *state* owns all public lands within its borders—drafted a letter based on extensive research and analyses of the U.S. Constitution, state statutes, case law and public documents. Carver then sent copies of the letter to Nevada's governor and Interior Secretary Babbitt, Agriculture Secretary Mike Espy and several other department heads in Washington, D.C.. Riding a groundswell of local support, the Nye County Board of Commissioners adopted a sweeping resolution, which became the flagship for ranchers and miners and elected officials from border to border across Nevada.

The official "Resolution 93-48" has become a prototype for other elected boards of county commissioners and supervisors to study and adapt to suit their own needs and circumstances. It recognizes that:

> . . . *the State of Nevada owns all public lands within the borders of the state of Nevada and the Counties of Nevada have a duty to manage these lands, to protect all private rights held on these lands, and to preserve local customs, culture, economy and environment.*

It further resolves that the Nye County commissioners are upholding their oathes of office by recognizing that within the borders of the state, " . . . *NEVADA OWNS ALL PUBLIC LANDS.*"

Every state has statutes that are nearly

interchangeable with the Nevada Revised Statutes enumerated in Resolution 93-48. Most Enabling legislation preceding statehood did not differ greatly from state to state. Much of this resolution could be used in other states of the West by simply changing the names of the county and state involved. What has become known as the "Nevada Plan" in Nevada could very well be the "Arizona Plan" or "Wyoming Plan" or "Utah Plan" if undertaken in those states.[57]

Dick Carver's initial letter in November of 1993 caused enough concern in Washington, D.C., that Interior Secretary Babbitt traveled quickly to Nevada in an effort to defuse this unique challenge to federal supremacy. He failed.

In March of 1994, Alaska's Lieutenant Governor John Coghill wrote to Carver: "I believe that your research needs greater exposure, and the message sent out to the people of this nation. If Congress and the Executive branch of the Federal Government are going to bankrupt us with their spending policies, we had better be ready to 'call in the loan,' and get our land back into the hands of sovereign individuals."

On March 8, 1995, The U.S. Justice Department filed a lawsuit in federal court in Nevada seeking to reaffirm " . . . *its ownership of and management authority over federal lands within Nye County, Nevada.*" Kathryn

---

57-Copies of Dick Carver's letter to state and federal officials and "Resolution 98-43" (and additional information on state sovereignty with regard to ownership of public lands) may be obtained from: Richard L. Carver, HCR 60 Box 5400, Round Mountain, NV 89045. (702) 377-2175.

Landreth, U.S. Attorney for the District of Nevada, justified the action by characterizing the Nye County commissioners as naughty children disobeying a figure of authority: "We cannot let county officials use their offices to violate the law and mislead their constituents regarding federal law. The actions of county officials could serve to incite further inappropriate behavior."

Carver welcomed the action. He felt that Landreth's comments illustrated the arrogance of most ranking federal officials. (God forbid that a lowly county official might challenge the supremacy of the Almighty Federal Government!) Carver pointed to the lawsuit where U.S. attorneys petitioned:

> . . . *to eliminate this dispute over the United States' title and management authority, a judicial declaration should be entered decreeing that the United States owns and has authority to administer the unappropriated public lands and National Forest System lands within Nye County, Nevada.*

He said if the federal agencies had any clear title or authority over the land, the lawyers would not have asked the court to establish that for them.

The suit came before federal District Court in Las Vegas in late July. After mid 1995, the case endured a dazzling choreography of legal maneuvers with federal attorneys on the defensive (a position from which victory is difficult). The Justice Department petitioned to have the State of Nevada brought in as a party to the suit. Nye County asked that other counties be allowed as interveners.

Carver says the case will ultimately be decided in the U.S. Supreme Court, and he is not displeased with that.

A philosophy similar to that of Dick Carver became the embodiment of an organization called the County Alliance to Restore the Economy and Environment (CAREE), founded in 1993. The organization came to life as the only *county-based* organization advocating state and local sovereignty of public lands and private property throughout the United States. CAREE quickly picked up momentum, spreading into a dozen states from Tennessee to Oregon.

CAREE became a lobbyist for property rights and a "research group" focusing on federal jurisdiction and paramount title. The group claimed "federal lands" are different from "public lands." It said the Constitution shows that federal lands over which the U.S. Government has jurisdiction are only those legally purchased with consent of the states within which they lie. By spreading this philosophy county-by-county across the nation's 3,048 counties, CAREE believed it could establish a nationwide infrastructure to assert state and local management and control over activities on all "public" lands.

CAREE emphasized that it was *not* against federal laws or environmental protection; it was *not* a fee-based organization (membership was free, but contributions were encouraged); it was *not* partisan—Republican or Democrat, conservative or liberal; and it was *not* a tax-exempt organization demanding special privileges while asking the "privilege giver" (Federal Government) to comply with constitutional laws.

CAREE used the Freedom of Information Act (FOIA) as an effective legal tool. In one incident, elderly residents of Boulder Oaks Resort—a trailer park within the Cleveland National Forest near San Diego, California— were ordered by U.S. Forest Service rangers to vacate their homes. After submitting a series of FOIA inquiries to the Department of Agriculture demanding proof of authority to remove the residents of the park, CAREE secured an order requiring the rangers to stop their actions at Boulder Oaks Resort. The federal agency was unable to produce any documentation to support its claim of jurisdiction or legal ownership of the property within the Cleveland National Forest.

A similar case involved a Nevada miner operating a legally-filed claim located on public acreage outside Las Vegas. Again using FOIA requests, CAREE secured the return of mining equipment seized by the Bureau of Land Management. The BLM could not show that it "owned" the property legally claimed by the miner. The Federal Government admitted its lack of jurisdiction and authority to seize the private property of the miner.

By December of 1994, CAREE had prepared for circulation to all the counties of the nation a sweeping, 20th century-style declaration of independence. It addressed the oppressive nature of the Federal Government in land-jurisdiction issues very much in the spirit of the Founding Fathers standing up to King George III. The "Petition to the 104th Congress of the United States for Redress of Grievances and Demand for Action" was designed for adoption by counties in every state—only the blanks needed filled in with the proper name of state.

While the document may not have been an exercise in textbook grammar, its purpose was clear. What effect would there be in the bureaucracies of Washington or in the Congress if signed copies of this document showed up from half the counties of the nation? Would it serve as a wake-up call? Again, the loudest voice is the one that gets heard—in this case, the voice of a united front.

CAREE organizers emphasized that no wording be changed in the original Petition, that copies be circulated and used in the various counties by simply filling the blanks with the appropriate names. This would build a unified army of CAREE supporters.[58]

Individual citizens can support CAREE principles in several ways. Upon request, a CAREE team will visit local communities to explain the issues in detail and demonstrate how to use the Freedom of Information Act to force federal officials to comply with other laws. Individuals can become active in informing the media and local government officials, circulating CAREE petitions and bringing information about wrongful trespassing by federal agents and agencies, as well as improper intervention into property and individual rights issues, to CAREE representatives.

58-For a copy of "Petition . . . for Redress of Grievances and Demand for Action" and more information on CAREE: County Alliance to Restore the Economy and Environment, 1350 East Flamingo Road, Suite 519, Las Vegas, NV 89119. (702) 796-8736. Ed Presley, National Director.
Or: County Alliance to Restore the Economy and Environment, 1025 16th Avenue South, Nashville, TN 37212. (615) 329-1516. Chuck Glaser, Director of Public Relations.

Of course, the CAREE Petition may be used as a model to create another. The language might be adjusted, tightened or reconstructed to fit a different group or organization. References to the 104th Congress could easily be replaced with another congress, with a state legislature or, in some circumstances, a county body.

Meanwhile, a very strong movement reasserting the Tenth Amendment of the U.S. Constitution has taken hold across the country. It is led by Colorado Senator Charles Duke, known widely as the father of the "Tenth Amendment Resolution." The premise is simple—as clearly stated in the Bill of Rights:

> *The powers not delegated to the United States by the Constitution, nor prohibited by it to the States, are reserved to the States respectively, or to the people.*

All the powers "*delegated to the United States*" are defined in Article I, Section 8, of the Constitution. Supporters of the Tenth Amendment Movement will accept nothing more or less. By mid 1995, more than 20 state legislatures across the nation had adopted the Resolution. Citizens and civic organizations in every state should encourage their elected state senators and representatives to support this return to constitutional government.[59] When the

---

59-More information about the Tenth Amendment Resolution may be obtained from: Senator Charles R. Duke, 1711 Woodmoor Drive, Monument, CO 80132-9002.

legislatures of 38 states (a three-fourths majority) have officially adopted the Tenth Amendment Resolution, it will go to the U.S. Congress as a referendum from the sovereign states that cannot be ignored.

Federal bureaucrats see the "states sovereignty" movement as a threat to their self-authorized omnipotence. The common objectives of Dick Carver, CAREE, the ranchers of Otero County, New Mexico, Senator Charles Duke and others, are to rein in the abuses of private property rights, to reduce government regulation for the sake of regulation, to control economy-bashing environmental overkill and to reassert civil liberties by limiting the powers of federal government as imposed by *un*elected bureaucrats.

On July 24, 1994, BLM rangers accosted a New Mexico family returning from a picnic and fishing outing near Santa Cruz Lake. An armed agent shot out a tire on the family vehicle and ordered everyone out of the car. The driver got out, his hands extended in a gesture of surrender, asking what he'd done wrong. The ranger maced the man before handcuffing him and his girlfriend. The girlfriend tried to lick the mace from the man's face. The ranger kicked her twice, then stomped the leg of the man's mother, breaking her ankle. After handcuffing the injured woman, the ranger maced the driver again. Children in the car cried hysterically. The ranger threatened to "blow their f--king heads off!" and pointed a shotgun at one of them. The arrival of a county deputy and a tribal police officer stifled a situation that might have gotten worse. The family was jailed without being told what they had done wrong. A U.S. magistrate released them because the BLM never produced a written complaint and no charges were ever filed. Neither was the officer disciplined.[60]

American citizens are offended by an attitude within the federal bureaucracies that they rule supremely and must answer to no one. Interior Secretary Babbitt epitomized the arrogance throughout his administration by implementing administratively anything he could not impose legislatively. The desire to rein in federal government is fired by endangered species enforcement destroying economies and livelihoods, by wetlands protection erasing property values—by envirocrats who do not care about constitutional rights or human relevance.

From 1964 to 1993, 34,000,000 acres of land were transferred from private ownership to the public domain. In 1964 only seven percent of federally-held property was severely restricted from public use; by 1993, *44 percent* of all so-called "public land" was off limits to most traditional public uses. Grassroots America cannot trust a government so bent on locking up the wealth of the nation in the "public interest" at the expense of life, liberty and pursuit of happiness.

In 1995 a strong sentiment surfaced among Republican members of the 104th Congress to hand over public holdings to the states. Determined to loosen the federal grip on hundreds of millions of acres, Representative

---

60-Details from local newspaper accounts and from a formal complaint filed in Santa Fe, NM, by an attorney for the family. Names and addresses are withheld in this version to protect the family from further recrimination.

Don Young of Alaska (Chairman of the House Resources Committee) advocated legislation to transfer to the states all authority over national parks, wilderness areas and wildlife refuges. Under the proposal, some of the land could even end up in *private* hands.

Utah Congressman James Hansen said, "One of the most prudent things we could do is turn over the [public] lands to the states. I honestly feel that would be a great thing for America."

True to form, however, the eco-preservationists shudder at the thought and offer crippled logic in response. Ben Beach of the Wilderness Society lamented, "It's going to be more difficult for local officials to resist a mining company that wants to work on public land."

So, why shouldn't a mining company work on public land? Is it undesirable only because it's a *mining* company? That's what the debate is all about—eco-groups and envirocrats choking off every effort to harvest and use the great wealth of this nation. Gross national product is affected by it. The trade deficit increases. The national debt flourishes. Thousands of families lose their incomes. Economies dry up. Towns die. The U.S. Government continues to be a government for the preservationists, of the preservationists and by the preservationists.

An array of plans is being considered to recover from regulatory suffocation with regard to property rights and lands uses. The Lake County, Oregon, Board of Commissioners has proposed *buying* federal forest lands from the U.S. Government. Neighboring Klamath County supports the idea.

Comprehensive county land use plans. The Nevada Plan. CAREE. Tenth Amendment. Federal legislation to turn public lands back to the states. Counties purchasing federally-held acreages and resources. Each approach is an effort to loosen the stranglehold of federal bureaucracies and uncompromising envirogroups. But the plans won't work without strong support and participation from the private sector.

Individuals owe it to themselves to find out the truth about the orchestrated destruction of property rights. Don't be led blindly down a path—by *anyone!* The federal regulating bureaucracies use convincing data (charts, graphs and studies) to support their actions publicly. Documents obtained through the Freedom of Information Act, however, often tell a much different story. The eco-groups have perfected an enormous propaganda machine to further their covert agendas. They don't want the real stories of real people suffering property rights abuses in the name of preservationism to be heard. No one should be satisfied with only one side of the story.

It's all about control—control of the people by controlling their land, water and resources. The constitutionally guaranteed right to own, manage and work property helped to make the freest nation in the world also the richest. The loss of property rights has resulted in severe curtailments of civil liberties and one of the largest national debts in the world.

It is not a battle for only by property owners and lands users. For Americans at large, the issue must be preservation of freedom. Without property, there is none.

Allodial Tenure and Title

"A right to property is founded in our natural wants, in the means with which we are endowed to satisfy these wants, and the right to what we acquire by those means without violating the similar rights of other sensible beings."
—Thomas Jefferson
3rd U.S. President, 1816

A common perception of "allodial title" is that it protects the landowner from all forms of external intrusion or harassment—including taxes and liens. This may or may not be the case. The 1880 edition of John Bouvier's congressionally authorized *Law Dictionary* defines "Allodium" as "*An estate held by absolute ownership, without recognizing any superior to whom any duty is due on account thereof.*" That definition is then "qualified" by a process of legal evolution:

In the United States the title to land is essentially allodial, and every tenant in fee simple has an absolute and unqualified dominion over it; yet in technical language his estate is said to be in fee, a word which implies a feudal relation, although such a relation has ceased to exist in any form, while in several of the states the lands have been declared to be allodial.

Remember, this definition by Bouvier was published in 1880. Most contemporary dictionaries only briefly allude to the term. Bouvier also wrote about "Tenure":

> *In the earlier ages of the world the condition of land was probably* allodial, *that is, without subjection to any superior,—every man occupying as much land as his necessities required and which he found unappropriated. Over this he exercised an unqualified dominion; and when he parted with his ownership the possession of his successor was equally free and absolute. An estate of this character necessarily excludes the idea of any tenure, since the occupant owes no service or allegiance to any superior as the condition of his occupation. But when the existence of an organized society became desirable, to secure certain blessings only by its means to be acquired, there followed the establishment of governments, and a new relation arose between each government and its citizens,—that of protection on the one hand and dependence on the other,—necessarily involving the idea of service to the state as a condition to the use and enjoyment of land within its boundaries. This relation was of course modified according to the circumstances of particular states; but throughout Europe it early took the form of the feudal system.*

The Founding Fathers recognized the inequities and limitations created by the feudal system of land tenure. They believed their fledgling republican government could not exist without unfettered ownership of private land. They established the allodial system of land tenure, under which ownership was free of all encumbrances.

George Gordon, a Common Law scholar in Isabella, Missouri, says true allodial tenure and title existed in the United States for only 33 years—from 1787 to 1820. He says after the U.S. acquired the Louisiana Purchase, lawmakers had to do something that would allow them to sell the land (because nothing in the Constitution would allow them to *own* it in the first place). They passed the Land Patent Act of 1820. The concept of allodial tenure and title began then to revert to a system of feudalism in which the state owns the land. Government "owned" the land and patented it. Counties began taxing it for improvements to roads. Gordon says a perverted version of allodial title existed from 1820 to 1837, when the Land Patent Act was amended. The amended Act gave way to the Homestead Act of 1862. At that time the government claimed "ownership" to millions of acres it planned to sell to people who would fulfill certain obligations to take possession.

Another view has it that allodial titles were *reaffirmed* in 1820 with the enactment of the Land Patent Act. The belief is rooted in the language of the Act itself:

> *. . . to shield the present settlers upon public lands from merciless speculators, whose cupidity and avarice would unquestionably be tempted that the improvements which settlers have made with the sweat of their brows, and to which they have been encouraged by the conduct of government itself; for, though they might be considered as embraced*

> *by the letter of the law which provides against intrusion on public land, that it was calculated to plant in the new country a population of independent, unembarrassed freeholders . . . "*

Supporters of this conviction believe all the land transferred from the British Crown to the sovereign United States Government under the 1783 Treaty of Paris, and all the land acquired since by other treaties, enjoyed the freedom of allodial title. Nevertheless, an act of Congress created "land patents" in 1820 and the rest may be a matter of interpretation. Does "allodial title" mean "land patent," or are they two different things?

Simply stated, the Land Patent Act of 1820 upheld that farmers granted title to land under that law could not use that land as collateral for loans. President Lincoln applied the same idea to lands in the western reaches of the country under the Homestead Act of 1862. The land patent, therefore, is a conveyance of title known as Legal Title at Law. A Federal Land Patent is a Legal Title at Law. Any other paperwork purporting to grant title—even a court decree—is only an "appearance of title" and is superseded by Title At Law. Any land obtained by treaty within the United States is subject to treatment under the Land Patent Act and ownership may be secured by Legal Title At Law—or Federal Land Patent (FLP).

Carol Landi is a San Francisco-based legal researcher with a Stanford University background. She has become recognized as an expert on the topic of FLPs. She points out initially that the entire land area of the United States was acquired through treaties with other countries—the Treaty of Paris (original 13 colonies, 1783); Treaty of Peace with Great Britain (land westward to the Mississippi, 1783); the Treaty of Cession (the Louisiana Purchase, 1803); the Oregon Treaty of 1846; the Treaty of Guadalupe Hidalgo of 1848, and so on. The *first* FLP was issued to a man named John Martin on a parcel of land in New York City, March 4, 1788.

According to Landi, Treaty Law is supreme law. Land ownership protected by a Federal Land Patent under Treaty Law supersedes all other law (including the Constitution) and cannot be manipulated or harassed by state or federal courts. Therefore, says Landi, anyone obtaining an FLP should learn the Treaty Law that applies to that state. Hidalgo Treaty Law in California might differ from Cession Treaty Law in Kansas. Every protection a landowner needs is in that treaty. Judges cannot touch property protected by Treaty Law. Any litigation on FLP-protected land is fodder for the U.S. Supreme Court, which *must* find in favor of the landowner.[61] Logically, then (and *legally*), no one can make any claims against land protected with a Federal Land Patent unless those claims were made during the land patent proceedings.

Landi says one problem may lie in getting the FLP recognized. A "sandwich" of documents is necessary. First,

---

61-The U.S. Supreme Court decided in April, 1984, (*Summa Corporation v. State of California*) that California had made no claim of interest in the Bailona Lagoon at the time Summa had pursued patent proceedings, and no mention was made of any California interest in the patent that was issued to Summa. The Court said, " . . . [the interest] *must have been presented in the patent proceedings or be barred.*"

on the bottom of the sandwich is the Federal Land Patent. Over that is a Declaration of Land Patent. And on the top is the standard deed to the property, whatever its form—warranty deed, quit claim or otherwise.

The Declaration of Land Patent is a document essential to recognizing an FLP. A standard form is available from land patent offices or through land patent attorneys. If properly prepared and notarized, a legal letter will work. It must contain some specific information—a legal description of the property and references to the state constitution as a basis for filing—and it must be filed under "Real Estate" at the local courthouse. Filers must have the documents signed, dated, notarized and labeled with an itemization of any attachments (FLP, Declaration of Homestead, etc.) or county recorders may refuse to file the Declaration.

To obtain an FLP, landowners must follow a few basic steps:

(1) Obtain a copy of the legal property description from the warranty deed (or other) currently held on the property. It must contain a Township number, Range Number and Section number.

(2) Send or take the legal description to the Bureau of Land Management Office for the area in which the land is located. Do not send the actual warranty deed (or other), only a copy containing the legal description.

(3) Attach or present a letter requesting "a certified copy of the original land patent or land grant" covering the land

described. The copy must be certified.

(4) The cost of obtaining the land patent may vary from state to state, may be influenced by the amount of acreage, or may rise with time, but be prepared to pay for the certified copy. If working by mail, enclose a postal money order (*not cash or check*) of $25. Allow about six weeks for return of the patent papers. The BLM will refund any overpayment.

(5) Upon receipt of the land patent documentation from the BLM, record (file) it with the Declaration of Land Patent at the local courthouse in the county where the property is located.

(6) Federal Land Patent protection is now in effect.

City lots as well as rural acreages can be patented. The same basic information is necessary. Range and Township numbers are obtainable from the city engineer. A total legal description of the lot/property is essential. Declarations of Homestead may be done quickly and simply through the county recorder's office. Contact a land patent office or land patent attorney in the nearest major city (usually at the Federal Office Building) or a BLM District Office for certified land patent information. Then record the Declaration of Land Patent with the certified FLP and Declaration of Homestead, labeling the FLP and Homestead Declaration as "Exhibit A" and "Exhibit B" respectively. Ask that the registrar of deeds or county recorder record these documents in the "Real Estate" file.

This form of allodial title (FLP) is, by the very nature of the law that created it, a protection from foreclosure. The argument is that land cannot be foreclosed upon when it may not be used legally as collateral. When a Federal Land Patent is held by the landowner, then the bank or other institution initiating the foreclosure can never offer or guarantee a *clear* title to that land. No assurance of ownership goes with the purchase of such foreclosed land. Carol Landi says, "I would have no compunctions about even IRS auctioning off my land . . . as long as I have that patent recorded on it . . . I can challenge the new buyer that IRS didn't guarantee *clear* title, and that I still own my land. . . . even IRS cannot supersede federal treaty law or the provisions of any treaty of this country."[62]

Under the federal Land Patent Act, an FLP issued by the Bureau of Land Management, Department of Interior, of the United States Government, is the highest and best Title At Law. The holder of a Declaration of Land Patent, as an Assign, is the absolute owner of that property. No court can change a Declaration of Land Patent without the express permission of the holder of that Patent. A Declaration of Land Patent is superior to any other type of deed—warranty deed, sheriff's deed, etc. Once a

---

62-All of the information attributed to Carol Landi was found in an interview with *Acres U.S.A.* newsletter, a copy of which is preserved in the author's files. More information: Acres U.S.A., PO Box 9547, Kansas City, MO 64133; PIN Newsletter, PO Box 272, Hales Corner, WI 53130: and/or Family Farm Preservation, PO Box 287, Tigerton, WI 54486.

Declaration of Land Patent is duly in place, it cannot be removed.

The only authority responsible to the holder of a Declaration of Land Patent is the U.S. Government. A Patent cannot be violated or transferred by foreclosure, sheriff's auction or any other means without permission of the Assigns. Enforcement of a Patent must come from the U.S. Government. Should a Patent be violated, the Assign must file charges (criminal trespass, civil violations, fraud) with the Justice Department of the U.S. Government— namely, the U.S. Attorney General.

If a sheriff's sale should occur, the sheriff should be notified then that he is legally bound to advise each bidder that a Declaration of Land Patent exists in the name of the Assign; that a Declaration of Land Patent is the highest and best Title At Law; when the "sale" is complete, the land can never be resold; a "warranty deed" can never be drafted on the property; the buyer can never obtain a mortgage against the land; title insurance cannot be obtained for the property; a Declaration of Land Patent "clouds" title of the land *forever*; the successful bidder will not get possession of the property; the Declaration of Land Patent forbids ejectment of the Assign; and, a "sheriff's deed" and other documents pertaining to the sale constitute evidence of criminal trespass and fraud charges that will be filed with the U.S. Attorney General.[63]

63-No information presented in this book is meant to be construed as legal advice. Specific questions in the area of allodial titles and federal land patents should be directed to a land patent attorney.

A Federal Land Patent may not exclude the landowner from having to pay property taxes. Common Law expert George Gordon says so-called "property tax" is really an "ad valorem tax"—a tax not on the land, but on the *value* of the land. He says county assessors don't say, "We are going to charge you three dollars an acre for 100 acres and that is $300 per year." That would be *property* tax. Instead, the county fixes a levy based on assessed *value*. It becomes a tax on value—not property.

Gordon says there is a theory that landowners can take their lands off the tax rolls. He says, to his knowledge, it hasn't been done, but the theory might have some validity. If so, landowners would have to do it under the First Amendment's Free Exercise Clause and under old Common Law rules. Although allodial tenure and title laws remain on the books in most states, the system of property ownership has reverted to "feudalism." Gordon says, "That's what everybody wants [because] they don't know anything else."[64]

Typically, the consequences for failure to pay property taxes are confiscation of the property and disposal by sheriff's auction. However, the same supremacy of a Federal Land Patent *should* apply to this type of "foreclosure" proceeding.

It waits to be tested.

64-George Gordon's contribution to this material is contained in a recorded interview with the author, a cassette copy and transcript of which are preserved in the author's files. Additional information: George Gordon's School of Common Law, PO Box 297, Isabella, MO 65676.

To Be an Activist

"Let the people have property and they will have power—a power that will forever be exerted to prevent the restriction of the press, the abolition of trial by jury, or the abridgement of any other privilege."

—Noah Webster
American educator (1758-1843)

Every person who believes in the preservation of American freedom should be an activist. People tend to think in narrow terms and that can be counterproductive. In other words, someone restricted in the use of his farm in Iowa becomes very focused on wetlands or whatever the immediate problem may be, but may not pay much attention to the landowner in Oregon who cannot cut his own trees. Snowmobilers locked out of a national forest rally only for *their* access to the forest. Ranchers do not relate to national park encroachment on private property in Virginia. A Sierra Club lawsuit over telescope construction in Arizona should be a matter of concern to coastal developers in South Carolina.

It's all about property rights and the intelligent use of so-called "public" lands. It's all about freedom from litigious and bureaucratic usurpations. It's about preserving the "unalienable" rights of free Americans. One freedom lost is a threat to all the others. The right to property is equal to the right to life. In this context a tiny city lot becomes as important to the structure of American freedom as a 100-section ranch. The ability to *use* property in America equates to preservation of free enterprise and competitiveness in the world marketplace.

Everyone should be an activist. Some can do more than others. Some may write letters or make phone calls while others travel, address large gatherings and organize educational events. Those who write letters to editors play as intricate a role as those who lobby Congress. A housewife challenging a lopsided environmental curriculum at her children's school is just as vital as the land-rights organization churning out news releases and faxes to the media.

Activists should learn to use the same tools as their opposition. Mainstream media are flooded with *mis*information from envirogroups and government agencies. Advocates of property rights and public lands uses should never let a day pass without sharing the "truth" with local and national news sources. Lobbyists represent the special interests of eco-socialists and interventionists on Capitol Hill. Property rights groups have the same opportunity. Environmental legal defense funds file lawsuits willy-nilly to disrupt development and production. Those suffering the losses should file legal damage claims against those who *cause* the losses—the organizations *and the individuals,* including government officials. Activists should get involved with other activists and groups (Sierra Club has no qualms about joining Audubon in a common effort), because there *is* strength in numbers.

A LAND RIGHTS TOOLBOX

One of the strongest and most active organizations is the American Land Rights Association (ALRA), headquartered in Battle Ground, Washington. Every other land rights-oriented group or individual should somehow get connected with ALRA. Formerly known as the National Inholders Association, the organization offers a "Land Rights Toolbox" to all interested participants. It includes:

(1) **Full-time Washington, D.C., office and staff . . .**
to lobby Congress while keeping tabs on federal regulatory agencies. ALRA provides Washington, D.C., representation to many smaller groups.

(2) **Grassroots organizing**
ALRA will help local groups organize into more effective voices for property rights.

(3) **Day-to-day consulting . . .**
for private property owners and inholders threatened by new local regulations or federal agents acting outside their legal authority.

(4) **Special events**
ALRA will help organize rallies, press conferences, meetings, demonstrations and other events that help to shape public policy and opinion. Creative ideas for influencing Congress or the federal bureaucracies are the raw materials ALRA can help develop into effective results.

(5) **Land rights fax network**

ALRA offers fax lists for sending messages. ALRA has *thousands* of fax numbers for most private property and land rights advocates and organizations in the country.

(6) **Land rights alerts**

A newsletter for periodic briefings on current issues and informed "alerts" to call land rights activists to action.

(7) **Multiple Land Use Review**

The ALRA news magazine published monthly covering private property and land rights issues.

(8) **Congressional Alert System**

ALRA has Congress on computer 24 hours a day. The ALRA Congressional Alert System can produce copies of newly-introduced legislation, the latest information from Congress, Congressional Record searches and vote summaries on given issues.

(9) **Information Central**

The ALRA Information Central can monitor the *Washington Post, New York Times*, Associated Press and other major newspapers on important issues. It can access the *Federal Register*. It has access to new laws and regulations. The service is available to all interested entities.

(10) **E-Mail Network**

Over 5,000 people make up the Land Rights Network on the Internet, Compuserve and other on-line computer services. An E-mail address is all it takes to join this system.

(11) **Congressional Directory**
All ALRA members receive a short Congressional Directory for keeping tabs on Senators and Congressmen.

(12) **Federal Land Users Data System**
ALRA has a data base of over 1,000,000 names and addresses of inholders and other private property owners. It is possible to target every mining claim owner, rancher, inholder or private property owner by zip code, state or congressional district to organize a political effort.

(13) **Speakers Bureau**
The ALRA can provide entertaining and informative speakers on many issues for meetings and events.[65]

Individuals who do not belong to organizations—and even those who do—can accomplish a great deal without ever leaving the confines of their homes. One effective method is letter-writing (discussed at some length later in this chapter), and another is telephoning. But there are right ways and *not*-so-right ways of conducting telephone activism.

65-The American Land Rights Association (National Inholders Association) National Headquarters is at: 30218 NE 82nd Avenue (PO Box 400), Battle Ground, WA 98604. (360) 687-3087. FAX (360) 687-2973.
The ALRA Legislative Office is at: 233 Pennsylvania Avenue SE, Ste 301, Washington, DC 20003. (202) 544-6156.
FAX (202) 544-6774. E-mail: alra@pacifier.com

HOW TO BE EFFECTIVE ON THE TELEPHONE

Telephone trees are important—where one caller calls five or ten other people, those people in turn call five or ten more and so on. This kind of "networking" can be especially productive if at least half of those calls are long distance—even out of state. Equally as important as calling other activists, voters and taxpayers is calling elected representatives in state and federal government. Lawmakers seldom tire of hearing from their constituents; it gives them an opportunity to continually campaign for their reelection. The quantity—and especially the *quality*—of constituents' calls have been known to reverse voting positions.

Some lawmakers form their own opinions based on some criteria other than constituent participation, but to most of them the voice of the voter is important. However, elected officials cannot read minds, nor do they often hear the private conversations that occur between family, friends and neighbors. They need direct contact.

A caller should never feel that his or her thoughts and concerns are unimportant. Every call is of value to the lawmaker, but some are more effective than others. The most productive calls follow a set of acceptable guidelines. Some easy rules to follow are:

(1) Thoughts and opinions should be organized, perhaps jotted down ahead of time, with nonessential verbiage deleted.

(2) One topic at a time with an emphasis in brevity.

(3) The caller should introduce himself (herself) at the start of the conversation and state the nature (issue) of the call. A caller representing a group or organization should say so and give its name and membership, a phone number and address for follow-up.

(4) Any personal experience or knowledge of an issue should be shared.

(5) Presentations should be tailored to fit the individual lawmaker's interests if possible.

(6) Calls about specific legislation should include the name and number of the bill or explicit content.

(7) The caller should be as specific as possible about why the legislation (issue) is objectionable and offer some recommendation for a particular stand or action.

(8) Discussion of technical information should be qualified with technical competence or expertise.

(9) Courtesy is the watchword; threats, direct or implied, are taboo.

(10) Timing is important. Calls should be placed to coincide with issues coming to debate in the lawmaking body.

(11) Expressions of thanks and continued interest should conclude each call.

(12) A follow-up call or letter should express appreciation for any lawmaker who acts (votes) in favor of a caller's recommendations. Elected officials don't often receive the praise they deserve for responding to constituents' concerns.

Telephoning is a form of lobbying. However, most lobbying is done in person by trained lobbyists representing the wishes of special interests. When individuals worried about property rights or other issues turn activist, they too represent the "special interests" of themselves, their organization or group. But lobbying elected representatives has been honed to an art. The inexperienced or untrained newcomer can be lost in a frenzy of procedure, proprieties and protocol.

THE EFFECTIVE GRASSROOTS LOBBYIST

As part of an "Activist 'How-To' Guide," former Congressman Mark Siljander of Michigan developed a set of grassroots lobbying techniques for The National Center for Public Policy Research. They include Five Initial Steps, followed by Seven Steps to Victory:

Five Initial Steps

(1) Identify the undecided Congressman or Senator.

(2) Identify the official's principle areas of interest or concern. That is, isolate factors that affect his/her decision-making process (i.e., find out if he/she is most responsive to

constituent interests, the media, business leaders, other politicians, the party leadership, emotional appeals, humanitarian concerns, or a combination of these and/or other factors).

(3) Recruit 25 registered voters in the official's district as your activist base—if you don't already have one. These activists can be recruited from civic groups, churches, political parties, etc.

(4) Educate these activists on the importance of the issue(s) and on the government measures they will be advocating. Make sure they fully understand their position and the arguments, both pro and con, so they can be effective advocates of their position.

(5) Ask each of these 25 activists to recruit three other family members, relatives, friends, co-workers and/or fellow church or community-group members to participate. They must live within the official's district and preferably be eligible to vote.

You now have an army of 100 people in the Congressman's or Senator's district.

Seven Steps to Victory

(1) Each activist should ask his/her three volunteers to call the Congressman's or Senator's *district* office to express their feelings on the particular issue. Activists should *not* use a script or risk revealing their calls are part of a

coordinated effort. Callers should simply ask in their own words for the Congressman/Senator to please consider their view and stress that they feel strongly about it. In addition (unless it is not true), callers should mention they are registered voters and never miss an election. They should give their names and addresses and ask the lawmaker's staff person to keep them posted on future activities concerning the issue.

It is most important that the activists contact their Senators' and Congressmen's *district* offices. The vast majority of calls to district offices come from people asking for assistance (with visas, Social Security problems, veterans' problems, etc.). Unlike Washington offices, the district offices seldom receive calls or letters from people expressing opinions. Thus, activists' calls directed to district offices will have a greater impact.

(2) Activists should use the information gathered on the principle areas of interest or concern of the lawmaker to benefit their own positions. For example, if the Senator/Congressman is most interested in property rights, then get the endorsement of leaders from the major property rights groups in his/her district. Always use the lawmaker's interests to further your own.

(3) Within three weeks of the massive phoning effort, you (the organizer) should arrange a meeting with the targeted lawmaker at his/her district office. No more than 12 of the activists should attend the meeting; more than that may be intimidating. Always remain sensitive to the lawmaker's position during the meeting, and each activist should be

prepared to present his/her views without repeating what others have said and without making threats. The idea is win someone over—not change a mind.

(4) Follow up after the meeting with a letter signed by all those who attended, thanking the lawmaker for his/her time. Also, send letters-to-the-editors of local newspapers thanking the lawmaker for his/her time and send copies of those letters—both as written and as published—to the lawmaker.

(5) The Senator/Congressman should be invited by the meeting attendees to attend a meeting on their terms. Within three weeks after the initial meeting, invite the lawmaker to speak to your activists on the particular issue. Turn-out is crucial. Your activists should have well-thought-out questions ready to ask the lawmaker—questions that pertain only to and reinforce your position. If possible, get the media to the meeting. This will apply a kind of unspoken pressure on the Senator/Congressman to adopt your position.

(6) Again, follow up the meeting with a "thank you" letter and letters-to-the-editors.

(7) Conduct a second round of phone calling, following the same procedure as before, as the congressional vote on your

issue draws near.[66]

Some individuals who foster very decided convictions on issues that affect them feel uneasy about lobbying and even more so about participating in public demonstrations. Just remember, the loudest voice is the one that gets heard. And the media *loves* a demonstration.

THE EFFECTIVE DEMONSTRATION

Imagine for a moment that you are a Congressman. Tomorrow your committee will vote on a bill that you believe most of your constituents support. You have not received much mail on the subject. You believe that while your constituents want you to vote for the bill, it's not critically important to them.

Presently, your Chief of Staff walks is and informs you that your district office just called and said, "The phones are ringing off the hook *against* this bill." As you digest this news, the district office calls again to say several dozen constituents have gathered outside and are picketing against the bill. While you ponder this development, your Chief of Staff (still on the phone) reveals that a reporter from the largest newspaper in your district is on the line wanting you to comment on the picket.

66-The National Center for Public Policy Research, 300 Eye Street NE #3, Washington, DC 20002. (202) 543-1286. FAX (202) 543-4779. E-Mail: ReliefRprt@aol.com

"Tell him there's no story," you say. "I'm not supporting the bill and the picketers are wasting their time." No one will ever know you were influenced by the demonstration outside your district office.

Why hold a demonstration?

There are five reasons why the most reluctant "activist" might wish to consider sponsoring or participating in a demonstration.

(1) A well-organized demonstration can attract valuable media attention. This attention can educate the public about your point of view, indirectly pressure public officials and increase the name identification of your group. This, in turn, enhances your ability to draw media attention in the future.

(2) A demonstration shows the public that many of their fellow citizens care strongly about a particular issue. Americans love to be on the winning side—the right side, the *American* side—so you'll sway many people to your view simply by pointing out that your position is a genuine and popular one.

(3) Demonstrations are great recruitment tools. By organizing such an event, others will be alerted to your group's existence and will seek you out to volunteer for your next project.

(4) A demonstration heightens the morale of your group. By working together on a successful event for a worthy

cause, you will improve the morale of your members and recruits and increase the likelihood that they will want to work together on future projects.

(5) A demonstration will help build your contact base.

Demonstration timing

Timing is crucial to the success of your demonstrations. Counter-demonstrations, for example, are best planned a half-hour to an hour *before* the demonstration you are countering. Except in special cases, it's easier to get press attention on weekdays than weekends and morning and early afternoon rallies are better than evening or late-night ones (reporters have deadlines). It's often a good idea to pick special holidays or anniversaries to enhance the significance of your demonstration. You'll also want to make sure your demonstration is somehow tied to the current public debate.

When to hold counter-demonstrations

When conducting a counter-demonstration within walking distance of the demonstration you are protesting, start your rally one-half to one hour *before* the opposition rally. Do not start with your top featured speaker. Assuming he/she is good, TV crews and reporters will wait a reasonable length of time before going to the other demonstration. Most media assignment desks will send only one reporter or crew to a location where two demonstrations are occurring within close proximity. Since your opposition will most likely start with their top featured speaker, placing your biggest-name speaker in the middle of your program will keep the media at your demonstration long after the opposition has fired its "big gun."

The advantage of pre-demonstration media hype

When organizing a counter-demonstration to an opposition rally you expect will draw considerable media interest, try to "scoop" the opposition by sponsoring newsworthy activities the *day before* the rallies. The media will often run "pre-demonstration" stories the day before an exceptionally large demonstration. But reporters frequently have difficulty finding a newsworthy angle for these stories and must resort to conducting pre-demonstration interviews or doing stories on the traffic problems anticipated at the rallies. Therefore, it is important to *provide* a newsworthy angle—such as an awards ceremony or a news conference featuring a well-known politician or celebrity.

Nine more important tips

(1) A picture is worth a thousand words. Make sure there are ample opportunities for the media to get *interesting* photos. Newspapers will often run photos with captions when there is no room for a lengthy story. Unique photo opportunities will attract television cameras.

(2) Every rally should have hand-held posters and signs. Make sure they are large and legible enough to be read and photographed from a distance. Use dark lettering over a

light background and always use short and to-the-point slogans.

(3)   Don't limit your photo opportunities to posters. A three-dimensional statue or figurine in a horse-drawn wagon, for instance, is a real attention-getter. A pig might represent "pork-barrel" spending; a scaled-down Statue of Liberty might help a cause related to civil freedom.

(4)   Special costumes and make-up can be effective tools for communicating specific messages. A 1993 rally by the activist group Putting People First challenged the position of a radical animal rights group by dressing as vegetables and chanting slogans like "Stop the murder, stop the pain, stop the slaughter of innocent grain." *New York Times*, MTV, the *Washington Times* and other major media covered the event.

(5)   Don't ruin a good rally with a poor sound system. Good speakers are ineffectual when an audience can't hear them.

(6)   Don't break the law. Always obtain permits when needed. Do not damage property. Don't litter and pick up all trash after an event.

(7)   Keep your demonstration concentrated in the area where it was designated to take place. A random crowd provides little excitement for news coverage. When asked by the media for an estimated number of attendees, shoot low. You don't want a news story on a disappointing turn-out. Always have "marshals" appointed within your group

to work crowd control. Never give the impression that your rally is anything but peaceful.

(8) Long before your rally, recruit support from other organizations and prominent individuals. This will add credibility to your effort.

(9) Always delegate responsibility. No matter the temptation, you can't do everything. Many people doing little jobs will bring together a better effort than one or two trying to do too much. Don't let any part of the program suffer for lack of attention. Surround yourself with motivated activists. Then delegate, delegate, delegate.[67]

Rallies, demonstrations and media coverage are effective methods of influencing public policy, just as telephoning and lobbying the policymakers. Another strong tool for promoting interest among elected officials for issues of concern among constituents is direct contact through the mail.

EFFECTIVE LETTERS TO CAPITOL HILL

Letters to policymakers—whether they are members of Congress or local elected officials—can be an effective means toward influencing public policy. Some letters, of

---

67-The National Center for Public Policy Research (footnote 65).

course, are more effective than others. There are some important guidelines to follow for constructing the best letters possible:

(1) Have a specific message

Make sure to have a "specific action" request *before* writing. If you want a decision changed, a vote cast a certain way or to communicate facts, be clear and concise. For legislative action, be sure to include the name and bill number of the legislation you are writing about (example: The Regulatory Transition Act, HR 450).

(2) Be brief

Letters are more likely read when they are short and to the point. Include one or two arguments for your position— presumably the arguments that you feel will be given particular weight by virtue of your position or those that are simply powerful on their own merits.

(3) Target your letters

Elected officials—particularly *federal* officeholders— seldom read their own mail. The burdensome duty usually falls to a staffer—often one with little influence over policy decisions. To increase the chances that your letters will have impact, direct them to staff members who have some responsibility for issues in question. For letters to Congress, address the envelopes to the Senators/Congressmen, then write "Attn: Legislative Assistant." You may prefer to write to the lawmakers' *district* offices. Washington offices overflow with mail, while district offices do not. A dozen letters in support of an issue at a district office might be perceived as a groundswell, while hundreds of letters to a Washington office might be scarcely noticed.

(4) **Personalize your letters**
Although mass-produced postcards and letters can show policymakers that many people hold the same point of view, individually written postcards and letters are much more effective. A policymaker knows the letter-writer is genuinely concerned about an issue if he/she sat down and crafted a personal message.

(5) **Use what you know about the official**
Before writing to the Congressman/Senator, take the time to learn what motivates him/her. Is he/she driven by a desire for reelection? Show how supporting your position would enhance his/her chances. Does he/she have a background in farming or ranching or other grassroots area? Appeal to him/her as a human being with feelings for the well-being of his/her constituents.

(6) **Be timely**
Write early if you want to influence a policymaker's opinion on a specific issue. Letters are most effective when received *before* the Senator/Congressman has formed his/her own opinion.

(7) **Be courteous**
Rude comments will have a negative effect. Standing firm on an issue does not require rudeness, threats or intimidation tactics.

(8) Follow up

If you receive a vague or seemingly obligatory response from an official, write again and request more specific information. If you receive a better response this time, send a "thank you." Notes of gratitude are few in Washington and, therefore, much appreciated.

(9) Utilize letters-to-the-editor and op/eds

If you get a letter-to-the-editor or an "opinion editorial" published, send copies with your letters to elected officials. This will demonstrate that you are more than casually interested in the issue and provide you with greater credibility.

(10) Sign your letters

Include your name, address and telephone number so policymakers can respond in whatever way they may choose.

(11) Type or print

Make sure your letters are legible by typing (word processing) them. If that is not possible, *print* them slowly and neatly. Do not write; do not make the person to whom you are writing have to "work" to read your letter.[68]

Well-funded environmentalist groups bent on shutting down industry, destroying rural economies, curtailing future development, restricting property rights

---

68-The National Center for Public Policy Research (footnote 65).

and locking up the unappropriated lands of the nation against all traditional uses by the public know they must present themselves to the urban masses in a favorable light. They must sell themselves as the protectors and saviors of wildlife and its habitat. They have developed a cunning and consistent propaganda machine that never stops providing "information" to the public through direct-mail fundraising campaigns, membership drives, magazine articles, television documentaries and a very *schmoozie* relationship with the media.

Grassroots activists must work to refine their own system of communicating with the media—whether it's television, radio or newsprint. Remember, the media often work with the material that *comes to them*, something they can respond to, something they know exists suddenly that they had no knowledge of before. The eco-groups keep themselves visible by remaining consistently present in mailboxes.

Grassroots activists with interests in preserving property rights and other basic liberties unique to the American Dream must learn to do the same. The "Activist 'How-To' Guide" includes some valuable information on crafting responsible and credible news releases.

WRITING EFFECTIVE PRESS RELEASES

There are some very specific formats for writing press releases. Those done properly are the ones that get noticed. It is to the advantage of the person or organization drafting the press release to know that its primary function is to efficiently transmit information, and so it becomes a strong tool for conveying a specific message (special interest, agenda, etc.).

Getting started

You must develop a "press release" letterhead. Styles vary, but a typical press release contains the name of an organization, its address and phone number on the top left corner of the page. The words "NEWS" or "PRESS RELEASE" or "MEDIA RELEASE" should appear on the top right. A standard press release will arrive on legal-size paper (8½ x 14), although standard (8½ x 11) size is also appropriate.

You will need a #10 (standard business size) envelope that matches your press release letterhead for style, ink and paper colors. Larger envelopes (manila) may be used for sending larger items (photos, books, etc.).

On the top of your release you must type "For Release: Immediate" or "For Release: (Date)." If you don't want the material used until a specified time, type "Embargoed Until (Date and Time)" after the "For Release." On the right, directly across from the "For Release" information, you should type "Contact:" and then the name(s) and telephone number(s) where journalists may obtain additional information or get questions answered.

The slug

The first piece of text in a press release is called the "slug." This is the name for the title or headline. It should summarize the topic in one brief phrase. Use action verbs to create excitement about a "news" story.

The inverted triangle

The best press release is drawn like an inverted triangle. If it were a symbol on a page, it would appear as ▼. The "inverted triangle" in a press release contains the biggest (most important) information at the top. The next paragraph should contain slightly less important information and so on. If written properly, the bottom *half* of the release could be torn off and journalists would still have sufficient information to do a story. The inverted triangle concept is important because journalists are busy, pushing deadlines; they don't have time to read every word of every release they receive. Don't waste your good information—the really important stuff—at the *bottom* of an inverted triangle.

The lead

Sometimes spelled "lede," this is the first sentence or paragraph of a press release. It must contain the *who, what, where, when* and *why.* This is the information a journalist needs to pursue your story. Make sure nothing is left out.

Style

Keep the release short and succinct. A press release should rarely exceed one page. Always type (word process) a release and use wide margins. Double-spacing is a good idea, allowing room for journalists' notes between lines. At least, leave some room between paragraphs. Paragraphs and sentences must be kept short and clear. Use exact dates (June 5 or Monday, June 5) rather than general terms (next Monday). In text, spell out numbers one through ten, then use numerals for larger numbers.

Objectivity

Again, press releases are meant to transmit facts. Opinions are not news unless they are solicited by a reporter. It's okay to include a quote by an important member of your group or a recognized name who supports you. Make sure the quote is clearly attributed to its source.

Closing symbols

A journalist will want to recognize the end of a press release (if he/she goes that far). There are two commonly-accepted symbols: one is "-30-" and the other is "###". Use either one at the end of your release, positioning it in the lower center of the page. In the rare case that a press release is longer than one page, the word "MORE" (also centered) should appear at the bottom of any page that is not the last page.[69]

69-The National Center for Public Policy Research (footnote 65). All of the information on Grassroots Lobbying, Organizing Demonstrations, Letters to Capitol Hill and Writing Press Releases was researched and prepared by the Center's Project *Relief* Grassroots Task Force, David Ridenour, Task Force Chairman.

Press releases are worthless if they don't see print or broadcast air time. Local newspapers and radio stations are good for promoting a cause within a small radius. That coverage is important. The contact information is available by looking up the various sources in a phone book. Treat local newspapers and radio and television stations the same as you would the major media sources elsewhere in the country. They all can help you with your message.

MAJOR MEDIA CONTACTS

Newspapers:

ASSOCIATED PRESS, 50 Rockefeller Plaza, New York, NY 10020. (212) 621-1500.

BOSTON GLOBE, PO Box 2378, Boston, MA 02107-2378. (617) 929-2000.

CHICAGO TRIBUNE, 435 N. Michigan Ave., Chicago, IL 60611. (312) 222-3232.

LOS ANGELES TIMES, Times Mirror Square, Los Angeles, CA 90053. (213) 237-5000.

MIAMI HERALD, One Herald Plaza, Miami, FL 33101. (305) 350-2111.

NEW YORK TIMES, 229 W. 43rd St., New York, NY 10036. (212) 556-1234.

PHILADELPHIA INQUIRER, PO Box 8263, Philadelphia, PA 19101. (215) 854-2000.

UNITED PRESS INTERNATIONAL, 1400 Eye St. NW, Washington, DC 20005. (202) 898-8000.

USA TODAY, 1000 Wilson Blvd., Arlington, VA 22209. (703) 276- 3400.

WASHINGTON POST, 1150 15th St. NW, Washington, DC 20071. (202) 334-6000.

WASHINGTON TIMES, 3600 New York Ave. NE, Washington, DC 20002. (202) 636-3000.

Magazines:

NEWSWEEK, 444 Madison Ave., New York, NY 10022.

TIME, Time/Life Bldg, Rockefeller Ctr, New York, NY 10020.

US NEWS & WORLD REPORT, 2400 N St. NW, Washington, DC 20037. (202) 955-2000.

Television Networks:

ABC TELEVISION NETWORK, 77 W. 66th St., New York, NY 10023-6201. (212) 456-1000.

CBS, INC., 51 W. 52nd St., New York, NY 10019-6101. (212) 975-4321.

NBC, 30 Rockefeller Plaza, New York, NY 10112-0100. (212) 664-4444.

FOX BROADCASTING COMPANY, 10201 W. Pico Blvd., Los Angeles, CA 90035. (310) 277-2211.

PBS - PUBLIC BROADCASTING SERVICE, 1320 Braddock Place, Alexandria, VA 22314-1649. (703) 739-5000.

CNN, Turner Broadcasting, One CNN Center, Atlanta, GA 30348.

Evening News:

ABC WORLD NEWS TONIGHT, 77 W. 66th St., New York, NY 10023. (212) 887-4040.

CBS EVENING NEWS WITH DAN RATHER, 524 W. 57th St., Studio 47, New York, NY 10019. (212) 975-4114.

NBC NIGHTLY NEWS, 30 Rockefeller Plaza, New York, NY 10112. (212) 664-4971.

MACNEIL/LEHRER NEWSHOUR, 356 W. 58th St. 5b, New York, NY 10019. (212) 560-3113.

News Programs:

ABC 20/20, 157 Columbus Ave., New York, NY 10023. (212) 456-2020.

ABC NIGHTLINE, 1717 De Sales St., Washington, DC 20036. (202) 885-7360.

ABC PRIMETIME, 1965 Broadway, New York, NY 10023. (212) 580-6199.

ABC THIS WEEK WITH DAVID BRINKLEY, 1717 De Sales St. NW, Washington, DC 20036. (202) 887-7375.

CBS 48 HOURS, 524 W. 57th St., 5th Floor, New York, NY 10019. (212) 975-4848.

CBS 60 MINUTES, 524 W. 57th St., New York, NY 10019. (212) 975-2006.

CBS NIGHTWATCH, 2033 M St. NW, Ste. 201, Washington, DC 20036. (202) 429-9679.

Morning News Programs:

ABC GOOD MORNING AMERICA, 77 W. 66th St., New York, NY 10023. (212) 496-4800.

CBS THIS MORNING, 524 W. 57th St., Ste. 44, New York, NY 10019. (212) 975-2824.

NBC TODAY, 30 Rockefeller Plaza, New York, NY 10112. (212) 664-4444.

FOX MORNING NEWS, 5151 Wisconsin Ave. NW, Washington, DC 20016. (202) 244-5151.

CNN LARRY KING LIVE, 820 First St. NE, Washington, DC 20002. (202) 898-7900.

Cable Television:

BLZ NET/AMERICAN BUSINESS NETWORK, US Chamber of Commerce, 1615 H St. NW, Washington, DC 20062. (202) 463-5690.

CBN CHRISTIAN BROADCASTING NETWORK, 1301 Pennsylvania Ave. NW, Ste. 403, Washington, DC 20004. (202) 638-4734.

CNN, One CNN Center, Atlanta, GA 30348-5366. (404) 827-1500.

C-SPAN, Viewer Services, 400 N. Capitol NW #650, Washington, DC 20001-1511.

THE DISCOVERY CHANNEL, 8201 Corporate Dr., Landover, MD 20785. (301) 986-1999.

INDEPENDENT NETWORK NEWS, Programming, 200 E. 42nd St., New York, NY 10017. (212) 210-2411.

PUBLIC AFFAIRS TELEVISION, 356 W. 58th St., New York, NY 10019.

TNT/IBS, Programming, 150 Techwood Dr. NW, Atlanta, GA 30348-5264. (404) 827-1500.

USA CABLE NETWORK, Programming, 1230 Avenue of the Americas, New York, NY 10020. (212) 408-9100.

Radio:

ASSOCIATED PRESS BROADCAST SERVICES, 1825 K St. NW, Washington, DC 20006-7200. (202) 955-7200.

NATIONAL PUBLIC RADIO, 2025 M St. NW, Washington, DC 20036. (202) 722-2000.

PACIFICA NATIONAL NEWS SERVICE, 702 H St. NW, Washington, DC 20001.

UPI RADIO NETWORKS, 1400 I St. NW, 9th Floor, Washington, DC 20005.

PAUL HARVEY NEWS AND COMMENT, 333 N. Michigan @ Paul Harvey Dr., Chicago, IL 60601. (312) 899-4085. FAX (312) 899-4088.

THE LARRY KING SHOW, 1755 S. Jefferson Davis Hwy, Arlington, VA 22202. (703) 685-2075.

RUSH LIMBAUGH, EFM Media Mgmt., 242 Madison Ave., Ste. 920, New York, NY 10173. FAX (212)613-3884.

You Are Not Alone

"Our social system rests largely upon the sanctity of private property; and that state or community which seeks to invade it will soon discover the error in the disaster which follows."

—William Henry Moody
U.S. Supreme Court Justice

Property owners and lands users often think in solitary terms—perhaps because they are accustomed to doing for themselves. They like to make their own decisions, take their own chances and learn from their own mistakes. Successes, then, when they come, are their own. Similarly, responsibility for their failures is also theirs. They are not accustomed to "joining" or leaning on anyone for support. It's the American spirit of independence—a liability, at times, as much as an asset. When a farmer is "regulated" out of business, he feels as though it's just he against the government. A logger out of work blames the species or environmental group that took *his* job.

Landowners feel overwhelmed when facing the National Park Service threatening to condemn their property. Most of them do not get "involved" until they themselves are affected by environmental overkill and bureaucratic regulation.

When an individual experiencing property rights abuses decides to fight back, he or she is already at a disadvantage. The agency or eco-group involved has probably become firmly entrenched over time without attracting much notice and the landowner is suddenly forced to take a *de*fensive position—a position from which no one has ever won a battle. *Off*ense wins. It's time to realize YOU ARE NOT ALONE!

There are at least 1,500 different organized groups—some large, some small—fighting for the causes of property rights, lands uses and personal freedom (the American Dream) within the shores and borders of this country. They represent farmers, industry, recreation, resource harvesters and all forms of property ownership. Every American concerned about the erosion of so-called "unalienable" rights should belong to one or more of these groups. They are excellent sources of information, often circulating newsletters. Their membership numbers are as important during the lobbying process as are those of Sierra Club. Maintaining membership or affiliation with several of them—within local communities and nationally—is usually not costly and contributes to a common union (strength in numbers) of varying property rights issues.

Organizations exist in every nook and cranny of the nation—some with many chapters, some small and fighting solitary battles. The following pages contain a sampling of groups and organizations located in each state. There are many more not listed here. Any activist serious about learning the issues and fighting for preservation of the U.S. Constitution (and the American Dream) should begin calling, writing letters or making contacts in other ways. Find the right groups and *participate!* Remember, the Farm Bureau is not just for farmers. Horsebacking clubs face the same problems as snowmobilers. Western-based groups welcome and encourage eastern membership. It's about freedom in America, and it's *everybody's* fight.

Alabama:

ALABAMA FOREST OWNERS' ASSOCIATION, INC., PO Box 104, Helena, AL 35080. (205) 663-1131. FAX (205) 663-1131.

ALABAMA FORESTRY ASSOCIATION, 555 Alabama St., Montgomery, AL 36104. (205) 265-8733.

STEWARDS OF FAMILY FARMS, RANCHES AND FORESTS, PO Box 70482, Montgomery, AL 36107. (205) 264-4237 or (205) 264-1878.

Alaska:

ALASKA FOREST ASSOCIATION, 111 Stedman St., Ste. 200, Ketchikan, AK 99901. (907) 225-6114. FAX (907) 225-5920.

ALASKA LOGGERS LEGAL DEFENSE FUND, PO Box 389, Hoonah, AK 99829. (907) 945-3628. FAX (907) 945-3533.

ALASKA MINERS ASSOCIATION, 501 W. Northern Lights Blvd. #203, Anchorage, AK 99503. (907) 276-0347. FAX (907) 278-7997.

ALASKA STATE SNOWMOBILE ASSOCIATION, PO Box 210427, Anchorage, AK 99521-0427. (907) 344-1928. FAX (907) 561-5802.

RESOURCE DEVELOPMENT COUNCIL FOR ALASKA, INC., 121 W. Firewood Lane, Ste. 250, Anchorage, AK 99503. (907) 276-0700. FAX (907) 276-3887.

Arizona:

ARIZONA CATTLEMANS ASSOCIATION, 1401 N. 24th St., Ste. 4, Phoenix, AZ 85008. (602) 267-1129.

ARIZONA MINING ASSOCIATION, 2702 N. 3rd St., Ste. 2015, Phoenix, AZ 85004. (602) 266-4416. FAX (602) 266-4418.

ARIZONA TRAIL RIDERS, PO Box 31877, Phoenix, AZ 85046. (602) 437-2394.

OUR LAND SOCIETY, 3911 E. Dover, Mesa, AZ 85205. (602) 985-0212. FAX (602) 924-4636.

Arkansas:

ARKANSAS FORESTRY ASSOCIATION, 410 S. Cross St., Ste. C, Little Rock, AR 72201-3014. (501) 374-2441.

CONCERNED CITIZENS COALITION, PO Box 95, Cove, AR 71937. (501) 394-3427. FAX (501) 387-2244.

California:

ALLIANCE FOR ENVIRONMENTAL RESOURCES, PO Box 849, Hayfork, CA 96041. (916) 628-5304.

ASSOCIATED CALIFORNIA LOGGERS, 555 Capitol Mall #745, Sacramento, CA 95814. (916) 441-7940. FAX (916) 441-7942.

CALIFORNIA ASSOCIATION OF 4WD CLUBS, 3104 O St. #313, Sacramento, CA 95816.

CALIFORNIA DESERT COALITION, 6192 Magnolia Ave., Ste. D, Riverside, CA 92506. (714) 684-6509. FAX (909) 684-2043.

CALIFORNIA FARM WATER COALITION, 717 K St., Ste. 510, Sacramento, CA 95814-3406. (916) 441-7723. FAX (916) 441-7842.

CALIFORNIA FORESTRY ASSOCIATION, 1311 I St., Ste. 100, Sacramento, CA 95814. (916) 444-6592. FAX (916) 444-0170.

CALIFORNIA MINING ASSOCIATION, One Capitol Mall, Ste. 220, Sacramento, CA 95814. (916) 447-1977. FAX (916) 447-0348.

CALIFORNIA OUTDOOR RECREATION LEAGUE, 35205 Johil Rd., Newberry Springs, CA 92365. (619) 257-3350.

CALIFORNIANS FOR CONSTITUTIONAL GOVERNMENT, PO Box 1107, Pleasanton, CA 94566. (510) 426-8756

EAST MOJAVE PROPERTY OWNERS ASSOCIATION, PO Box 103, Cima, CA 92323. (818) 956-0008. FAX (818) 353-4583.

FISHERMAN'S COALITION, 2405 E. Harbor Dr., San Diego, CA 92113. (619) 233-1633.

GOLD PROSPECTORS ASSOCIATION OF AMERICA, PO Box 507, Borsall, CA 92003. (619) 728-6620. FAX (619) 728-4815.

HIGH DESERT MULTIPLE-USE COALITION, 1163 S. Garth, Ridgecrest, CA 93555.

PACIFIC LEGAL FOUNDATION, 2700 Gateway Oaks #200, Sacramento, CA 95833. (916) 641-8888. FAX (916) 920-3444.

PACIFIC MINING ASSOCIATION, 2051 Pacific Ave., Norco, CA 91760. (909) 371-6493. FAX (909) 737-2508.

TAXPAYERS FOR ENVIRONMENT AND ITS MANAGEMENT (T.E.A.M.), PO Box 651, Fortuna, CA 95540-0651. (707) 764-5158.

Colorado:

COLORADO CATTLEMAN'S ASSOCIATION, Livestock Exchange Bldg., Ste. 220, Denver, CO 80216. (303) 296-1112.
FAX (303) 296-1115.

COLORADO MINING ASSOCIATION, 1340 Co. St. Bank Blvd., 1600 Broadway, Denver, CO 80202. (303) 894-0536. FAX (303) 894-8416.

COLORADO OFF HIGHWAY VEHICLE COALITION, PO Box 620523, Littleton, CO 80121-0523. (303) 866-3581.

COLORADO PROPERTY RIGHTS ASSOCIATION, PO Box 7031, Golden, CO 80403. (303) 985-0427.

COLORADO SNOWMOBILE ASSOCIATION, INC., PO Box 468, South Fork, CO 81154. (719) 873-5923.

COLORADO TIMBER INDUSTRY ASSOCIATION, PO Box 95, Lake City, CO 81235. (303) 944-2742.

COLORADO WOOL GROWERS ASSOCIATION, 211 Livestock Exchange Bldg., Denver, CO 80216. (303) 294-0854.
FAX (303) 297-1031.

MOUNTAIN STATES LEGAL FOUNDATION, 1660 Lincoln St., Ste. 2300, Denver, CO 80264. (303) 861-0244. FAX (303) 831-7379.

NATIONAL COALITION FOR PUBLIC LANDS AND NATURAL RESOURCES, 301 N. Main, Pueblo, CO 81003.
(719) 543-8421. FAX (719) 543-9473.
Note: Formerly known as Western States Public Lands Coalition and commonly called "People For the West," this organization has hundreds of chapters located across the nation.

PUBLIC LANDS ACCESS COALITION, 7146 S. Dexter Ct., Littleton, CO 80122. (303) 290-0164.

ROCKY MOUNTAIN OIL & GAS ASSOCIATION, 1860 Lincoln St., Denver, CO 80295. (303) 860-0099. FAX (303) 860-0310.

Connecticut:

ALLIANCE FOR AMERICA, PO Box 736, Waterford, CT 06385.
(203) 444-0434.
Note: This organization is really an umbrella from several hundred smaller groups. It has chapters in many states. The main office address is found in the New York listings.

Delaware:

DELAWARE FARM BUREAU FEDERATION, 233 S. DuPont Hwy., Camden, DE 19934. (302) 697-3183. FAX (302) 697-1428.
Note: The Farm Bureau has federation offices in every state and thousands of counties. The American Farm Bureau Federation office address is found in the Illinois listings.

District of Columbia:

AMERICAN FOREST COUNCIL, 1250 Connecticut Ave. NW #200, Washington, DC 20036.

AMERICAN MINING CONGRESS, 1920 N St. NW, Ste. 300, Washington, DC 20036. (202) 861-2800. FAX (202) 861-7535.

AMERICAN PROPERTY RIGHTS ALLIANCE, 1212 New York Ave.
NW, Ste. 1210, Washington, DC 20005. (202) 371-5566.

CITIZENS FOR THE ENVIRONMENT, 470 L'Enfant Plaza SW, Ste.
7401, Washington, DC 20024. (202) 488-7255. FAX (202) 488-8282.

DEFENDERS OF PROPERTY RIGHTS, 6235 33rd St. NW,
Washington, DC 20015. (202) 686-4197. FAX (202) 686-0240.

NATIONAL CATTLEMEN'S ASSOCIATION, 1301 Pennsylvania Ave.
NW, Ste. 300, Washington, DC 20004. (202) 347-5355.
FAX (202) 638-0607.

AMERICAN LAND RIGHTS ASSOCIATION, 233 Pennsylvania Ave.
SE, Ste. 301, Washington, DC 20003. (202) 544-6156.
FAX (202) 544-6774.
Note: Formerly National Inholders Association.

NATIONAL WETLANDS COALITION, 1050 Thomas Jefferson NW,
6th Floor, Washington, DC 20007. (202) 298-1879.

Florida:

AMERICAN ENVIRONMENTAL FOUNDATION, PO Box 7015,
Milton, FL 32570. (904) 626-1783.

CITIZENS FOR CONSTITUTIONAL PROPERTY RIGHTS, PO Box
757, Crestview, FL 32536. (904) 682-6156. FAX (904) 678-3321.

SOUTHEASTERN WOOD PRODUCERS ASSOCIATION, PO Box 9,
Hillard, FL 32046. (904) 845-7133. FAX (904) 845-7345.

Georgia:

FOREST FARMERS ASSOCIATION, 4 Executive Park East NE,
Atlanta, GA 30329. (404) 325-2954.

GEORGIA FORESRTY ASSOCIATION, INC., 500 Pinnacle Ct #505, Norcross, GA 30071-3634. (404) 840-8961.

GEORGIA MINING ASSOCIATION, 900 Circle 75 Pkwy., Ste. 1740, Atlanta, GA 30339. (404) 952-7975. FAX (404) 952-7986.

SOUTHEASTERN LEGAL FOUNDATION, 2900 Chamblee-Tucker, Atlanta, GA 30341. (404) 458-8313.

Hawaii:

ALLIANCE FOR AMERICA, 40 Aulike St., Ste. 311, Kailua, HI 96734. (808) 261-9120.

Idaho:

BLUE RIBBON COALITION, PO Box 5449, Pocatello, ID 83202. (208) 237-1557. FAX (208) 237-1566.

FREE ENTERPRISE LEGAL DEFENSE FUND, PO Box 44704, Boise, ID 83711. (208) 336-5922. FAX (208) 336-7054.

IDAHO CATTLE ASSOCIATION, 2120 Airport Way, Boise, ID 83701. (208) 343-1615.

IDAHO MINING ASSOCIATION, PO Box 1660, Boise, ID 83701. (208) 342-5003. FAX (208) 345-4210.

IDAHO PRIVATE PROPERTY COALITION, PO Box 15977, Boise, ID 83715-5977. (208) 344-2271. FAX (208) 336-9447.

Illinois:

AMERICAN FARM BUREAU FEDERATION, 225 Touhy Ave., Park Ridge, IL 60068. (312) 399-5746. FAX (312) 399-5896.

ILLINOIS ASSOCIATION OF SNOWMOBILE CLUBS, 2904 E. 24th Rd., Marseilles, IL 61341. (815) 795-2021.

ILLINOIS CATTLEMAN'S ASSOCIATION, RR 1 Box 15, Adair, IL 61411. (309) 653-2590.

ILLINOIS WOOD PRODUCTS ASSOCIATION, 115 W. Indian Trail, Aurora, IL 60506. (708) 897-5545.

NATIONAL TRAPPERS ASSOCIATION, PO Box 3667, Bloomington, IL 61702-3667. (309) 925-3022. FAX (309) 925-4122.

Indiana:

PROTECT PROPERTY RIGHTS, PO Box 323, Battle Ground, IN 47920. (317) 567-2750.

STOP TAKING OUR PROPERTY, PO Box 599, Chesterton, IN 46304. (219) 926-6315. FAX (219) 926-4651.

Iowa:

BASIC FREEDOMS, INC., 3405 Rochester Ave., Iowa City, IA 52240.

NATIONAL FARMERS ORGANIZATION, 505 Elwood Dr., Ames, IA 50010.

Kansas:

KANSAS GRASSROOTS ASSOCIATION, Rt. 5 Box 77, Emporia, KS 66801.

KANSAS LAND COALITION, RR 1 Box 212, Wakefield, KS 67487. (913) 461-5533.

Kentucky:

KENTUCKY LANDOWNERS ASSOCIATION, PO Box 425, Beaver Dam, KY 42320. (502) 274-4044.

Louisiana:

LOUISIANA SHRIMP ASSOCIATION, 2401 Manson St., Ste. C, Metiarie, LA 70002. (504) 885-7110. FAX (504) 885-6806.

LOUISIANA FORESTRY ASSOCIATION, PO Box 5067, Alexandria, LA 71307-5067. (318) 443-2558. FAX (318) 443-1713.

LOUISIANA LANDOWNERS ASSOCIATION, PO Box 44121, Baton Rouge, LA 70804-4121. (504) 927-5619. FAX (504) 928-7339.

SOUTHWEST LOUISIANA FISH ASSOCIATION, 712 Arthur Ave., Lake Arthur, LA 70549.

Maine:

ENVIRONMENTAL PERSPECTIVES, INC., 1229 Broadway, Ste. 313, Bangor, ME 04401-2503. (207) 945-9878.

MAINE CONSERVATION RIGHTS INSTITUTE, PO Box 220, Lubec, ME 04652. (207) 733-5593. FAX (207) 733-5593.

SMALL WOODLAND OWNERS ASSOCIATION, PO Box 926, Augusta, ME 04332. (207) 626-0005.

Maryland:

FAIRNESS TO LANDOWNERS COMMITTEE, 1730 Garden of Eden Rd., Cambridge, MD 21613. (410) 228-3822. FAX (410) 228-8357.

LAND RIGHTS LETTER, PO Box 568, Sharpsburg, MD 21782. (301) 797-7455.

MARYLAND LANDOWNERS ASSOCIATION, 202 High St., Cambridge, MD 21613. (301) 228-3610.

Massachusetts:

SNOWMOBILE ASSOCIATION OF MASSACHUSETTS, 28 Laurelwood Rd., Rutland, MA 01543. FAX (508) 886-2162.

WASHINGTON COUNTY ALLIANCE, 24 Orchard Rd., Concord, MA 01742. (508) 369-9308.

Michigan:

MICHIGAN FOREST ASSOCIATION, 1558 Barrington, Ann Arbor, MI 48103. (313) 665-8279.

MICHIGAN LANDOWNERS ASSOCIATION, 10025 Nashville Hwy., Vermontville, MI 49096. (517) 726-1253.

MICHIGAN SNOWMOBILE ASSOCIATION, 5181 Plainfield NE, Grand Rapids, MI 49505. (616) 361- 2285.

Minnesota:

CONSERVATIONISTS WITH COMMON SENSE, HC 1 Box 2673, Ely, MN 55731. (218) 365-3727.

MIDWEST FOUR WHEEL DRIVE ASSOCIATION, 2410 N.W. 15 ½ St., Faribault, MN 55021.

Mississippi:

COMMITTEE ON WETLANDS AWARENESS, 1418 20th Ave., Gulfport, MS 39501.

MISSISSIPPI FORESTRY ASSOCIATION, 620 N. State St. #201, Jackson, MS 39202-3398. (601) 354-4936.

Missouri:

CITIZENS FOR PRIVATE PROPERTY RIGHTS, Rt. 1 Box 429, Sullivan, MO 63080. (314) 627-3328. FAX (314) 627-2043.

MISSOURI LANDOWNERS ASSOCIATION, Rt. 1 Box 130, Huntsville, MO 65259. (816) 277-3125.

Montana:

COMMUNITIES FOR A GREAT NORTHWEST, PO Box 1320, Libby, MT 59923. (406) 293-8821. FAX (406) 293-4739.

MONTANA 4X4 ASSOCIATION, 2403 41st St. W, Billings, MT 59106. (406) 656-5509.

MONTANA MINING ASSOCIATION, 2301 Colonial Dr., Helena, MT 59601. (406) 443-7297. FAX (406) 443-7299.

MONTANA STOCK GROWERS ASSOCIATION, PO Box 1679, Helena, MT 59624. (406) 442-3420. FAX (406) 442-3420.

MONTANANS FOR MULTIPLE USE, PO Box 190068, Hungry Horse, MT 59919. (406) 387-5535. FAX (406) 387-4262.

PUTTING PEOPLE FIRST, PO Box 1707, Helena, MT 59624-1707. (406) 442-5700.

Nebraska:

NIOBRARA LAND OWNERS CONSERVANCY, RR. 2 Box 256, Ainsworth, NE 69210. (402) 387-2719.

Nevada:

COUNTY ALLIANCE TO RESTORE THE ECONOMY AND ENVIRONMENT, 1350 Flamingo Rd. #519, Las Vegas, NV 89119. (702) 796-8736.

NEVADA MINERS AND PROSPECTORS ASSOCIATION, PO Box 4179, Carson City, NV 89702. (702) 829-2148.

NEVADA MINING ASSOCIATION, 5250 S. Virginia St. #220, Reno, NV 89502-6046. (702) 829-2121. FAX (702) 829-2148.

NEVADA PUBLIC LANDS ALLIANCE, 17290 Sunbird, Reno, NV 89506. (702) 334-2772. FAX (702) 334-2770.

New Hampshire:

MULTIPLE USE ASSOCIATION, 332 North Rd., Gorham, NH 03581. (207) 836-2624. FAX (207) 836-2200.

NEW HAMPSHIRE LANDOWNERS ALLIANCE, PO Box 221, Campton, NH 03223. (603) 726-4025. FAX (603) 726-4308.

NEW HAMPSHIRE SNOWMOBILE ASSOCIATION, PO Box 38, Concord, NH 03302-0038. (603) 224-8906.

NEW HAMPSHIRE TIMBER OWNERS ASSOCIATION, 54 Portsmouth St., Concord, NH 03301. (603) 224-9699.
FAX (603) 228-0423.

New Jersey:

PINELAND LANDOWNERS DEFENSE FUND, PO Box 482, Chatsworth, NJ 08019.

New Mexico:

NEW MEXICO CATTLE GROWERS ASSOCIATION, 2231 Rio Grande Blvd. NW, Albuquerque, NM 87104. (505) 247-0584. FAX (505) 842-1766.

NEW MEXICO MINING ASSOCIATION, 4952 T.B. Catron NW, Albuquerque, NM 87114. (505) 897-0572. FAX (505) 842-0734.

PEOPLE FOR THE WEST - NEW MEXICO, 1207 Pecan Ave., Artesia, NM 88210. (505) 746-4734. FAX (505) 365-7671.

PUBLIC LAND USERS ASSOCIATION, PO Box 1990, Cuba, NM 87013.

New York:

ALLIANCE FOR AMERICA, PO Box 450, Caroga Lake, NY 12032. (518) 835-6702. FAX (518) 835-2527.

COALITION OF WATERSHED TOWNS, Sundown Rd., Sundown, NY 12782. (914) 985-7282. FAX (914) 589-9959.

NEW YORK STATE TIMBER PRODUCERS ASSOCIATION, PO Box 300, Boonville, NY 13309. (315) 942-5503.

PROPERTY RIGHTS COUNCIL OF AMERICA, PO Box 705, Warrensburg, NY 12885. (518) 696-2066. FAX (518) 696-5145.

PROPERTY RIGHTS FOUNDATION OF AMERICA, INC., PO Box 75, Stony Creek, NY 12878. (518) 696-5748.

North Carolina:

MULTIPLE USE COUNCIL, Rt. 3 Box 167, Sylvia, NC 28779. (704) 586-6353. FAX (704) 586-3197.

NORTH CAROLINA FORESTRY ASSOCIATION, 1600 Glenwood Ave., Ste. I, Raleigh, NC 27608-2355. (919) 834-3943. FAX (919) 832-6188.

NORTH CAROLINA LANDOWNERS ASSOCIATION, PO Box 1088, New Bern, NC 28563. (919) 633-5106.

North Dakota:

LANDOWNERS ASSOCIATION OF NORTH DAKOTA, RR. 1 Box 77, Lansford, ND 58750. (701) 259-2127.

Ohio:

CUYAHOGA VALLEY HOMEOWNERS ASSOCIATION, 3634 Oak Hill, Pennsylvania, OH 44264.

OHIO FORESTRY ASSOCIATION, 1335 Dublin Rd., Ste. 203D, Columbus, OH 43215. (614) 486-6767. FAX (614) 486-6769.

OHIO STATE SNOWMOBILE ASSOCIATION, 2466 Spore-Brandywine Rd., Bucyrus, OH 44820. (419) 562-2862.

Oklahoma:

OKLAHOMA LAND USERS ASSOCIATION, PO Box 1004, Idabel, OK 74745. (405) 286-7387.

Oregon:

ASSOCIATED OREGON LOGGERS, PO Box 12339, Salem, OR 97309. (503) 364-1330.

CITIZENS INFORMATION NETWORK, PO Box 1091, Ashland, OR 97520. (503) 488-2320. FAX (503) 488-2321.

COMMUNITIES FOR A GREAT OREGON - SWEET HOME, 28030 Meridian Heights, Sweet Home, OR 97386.

OREGON COTTLEMEN'S ASSOCIATION, SR. 1 Box 134A, Burns, OR 97720.

OREGON LANDS COALITION, 280 Court St. NE, Ste. 5, Salem, OR 97301. (503) 363-8582. FAX (503) 363-6067.

OREGONIANS IN ACTION, PO Box 230637, Tigard, OR 97281. (503) 620-0258. FAX (503) 639-6891.

SAVE OUR INDUSTRIES & LAND, HCR. 30 Box 11, Burns, OR 97720. (503) 573-6151. FAX (503) 573-3056.

WOMEN FOR MULTIPLE USE OF RESOURCES, 905 N. Bayshore Dr., Coos Bay, OR 97420.

Pennsylvania:

INDEPENDENT LANDHOLDERS ASSOCIATION, PO Box 57, Milanville, PA 18443. (717) 224-4666.

NATIONAL LANDOWNERS ASSOCIATION, Cradle of Freedom, 1427 Broad St., Philadelphia, PA 19147. (215) 271-1931.

ENNSYLVANIA FOREST INDUSTRY ASSOCIATION, PO Box 506, Kane, PA 16735. (814) 837-8944.

PENNSYLVANIA LANDOWNERS ASSOCIATION, PO Box 391, Waterford, PA 16441. (814) 796-3578. FAX (814) 796-6757.

Rhode Island:

EAST COAST FISHERIES FEDERATION, PO Box 649, Narragansett, RI 02882. (401) 782-3440. FAX (401) 782-3440.

South Carolina:

INTERMOUNTAIN FOREST INDUSTRY ASSOCIATION, 2040 W. Main St., Ste. 315, Rapid City, SD 57702. (605) 341-0875. FAX (605) 341-8651.

SOUTH DAKOTA MINING ASSOCIATION, 3801 S. Kiwanis, Ste. 5, Sioux Falls, SD 57105. (605) 332-3803. FAX (605) 344-1938.

Tennessee:

TENNESSEE CATLLEMAN'S ASSOCIATION, PO Box 906, Columbia, TN 38401.

TENNESSEE FORESTRY ASSOCIATION, PO Box 290693, Nashville, TN 37229. (615) 883-3832. FAX (615) 883-3832.

Texas:

FARM CREDIT PROPERTY RIGHTS FOUNDATION, PO Box 15919, Austin, TX 78761. (800) 452-6389.

HILL COUNTRY LANDOWNERS COALITION, 1002 Ash St., Georgetown, TX 78626. (512) 863-2935. FAX (512) 863-2935.

HOUSTON PROPERTY RIGHTS ASSOCIATION, 5075 Westheimer, Ste. 777, Houston, TX 77056-5606. (713) 224-4144. FAX (713) 227-4131.

RIVERSIDE & LANDOWNERS PROTECTION COALITION, INC., Rt. 2 Box 2505, Boerne, TX 78006. (512) 537-4830. FAX (512) 249-9037.

TEXAS & SOUTHWESTERN CATTLE RAISERS ASSOCIATION, 1301 W. 7th St., Ft. Worth, TX 76102. (817) 332-7064. FAX (817) 332-5446.

TEXAS FORESTRY ASSOCIATION, PO Box 1488, Lufkin, TX 75902-1488. (409) 632-8733.

TEXAS MINING AND RECLAMATION ASSOCIATION, 314 Highland Mall Blvd., Ste. 251, Austin, TX 78752. (512) 467-1300. FAX (512) 451-9556.

Utah:

COALITION OF RESPONSIBLE ENVIRONMENTALISTS, PO Box 704, Kanab, UT 84741. (801) 644-2937.

NATIONAL FEDERAL LANDS CONFERENCE, PO Box 847, Bountiful, UT 84011. (801) 298-0858.

UTAH CATTLEMENS ASSOCIATION, 150 S. 6th E. #10-B, Salt Lake City, UT 84102-1961. (801) 355-5748. FAX (801) 532-1669.

UTAH MINING ASSOCIATION, 825 Kearns Bldg., 136 S. Main St., Salt Lake City, UT 84101. (801) 364-1874. FAX (801) 359-7561.

WESTERN ASSOCIATION OF LAND USERS - GRAND COUNTY CHAPTER, PO Box 783, Moab, UT 84532. (801) 259-7425.

Vermont:

CITIZENS FOR PROPERTY RIGHTS, PO Box 393, Jonesville, VT 05466. (802) 434-2402.

LANDOWNERS UNTIED, PO Box 682, Newport, VT 05855. (802) 334-3400.

VERMONT PROPERTY RIGHTS CENTER, RR. 1 Box 8000, Underhill, VT 05489. (802) 899-4668.

Virginia:

CITIZENS FOR LAND RIGHTS, PO Box 1362, Culpepper, VA 22701. (703) 825-8275. FAX (703) 825-2948.

VIRGINIANS FOR PROPERTY RIGHTS, PO Box 986, Madison, VA 22727. (703) 948-7165. FAX (703) 948-7165.

Washington:

CENTER FOR THE DEFENSE OF FREE ENTERPRISE, 12500 N.E. 10th Place, Bellevue, WA 98005. (206) 455-5038. FAX (206) 451-3959.

GREAT NORTHWEST COALITION, PO Box 28151, Spokane, WA. (509) 326-2487. FAX (509) 326-2487.

AMERICAN LAND RIGHTS ASSOCIATION, PO Box 400, Battle Ground, WA 98604. (206) 687-3087. FAX (206) 687-2973.
Note: Formerly National Inholders Association.

NORTHWEST LEGAL FOUNDATION, 557 Roy St. #100, Seattle, WA 98109-4219. (206) 283-0503.

PROPERTY RIGHTS ALLIANCE, PO Box 985, Redmond, WA 98073. (206) 242-9569.

PUBLIC LAND USERS SOCIETY, 6824 19th W. #282, Tacoma, WA 98466. (206) 788-0162.

UNITED PROPERTY OWNERS OF WASHINGTON, PO Box 3336, Redmond, WA 98073.

WASHINGTON PRIVATE PROPERTY COALITION, 21604 N.E. Allworth Rd., Vancouver, WA 98604. (206) 687-2058. FAX (206) 687-2058.

Washington, DC:

DEFENDERS OF PROPERTY RIGHTS, 6235 33rd St. NW, Washington, DC 20015.

West Virginia:

ASSOCIATION OF NATURAL RESOURCE WORKERS OF WEST VIRGINIA, Rt. 12 Box 143, Ste. M13, Morgantown, WV 26505. (304) 594-2662. FAX (304) 594-2811.

Wisconsin:

LAKE STATE RESOURCE ALLIANCE, INC., PO Box 483, Hayward, WI 54843. (715) 634-3065. FAX (715) 634-5755.

PRIVATE LANDOWNERS OF WISCONSIN, 15930 Shady Hollow Lane, Woodman, WI 53827. (608) 533-3677.

PROTECT AMERICANS RIGHTS AND RESOURCES, HCR. 2 Box 171, Park Falls, WI 54552.

WISCONSIN WOODLAND OWNERS ASSOCIATION, PO Box 285, Stevens Points, WI 54481. (715) 341-4798. FAX (715) 346-3624.

Wyoming:

ABUNDANT WILDLIFE SOCIETY, 12665 Hwy. 59 N, Gillette, WY 82717. (307) 682-2626. FAX (307) 682-3016.

BUDD-FALEN LAW OFFICES, 204 E. 22nd, Cheyenne, WY 82001. (307) 632-5105.

WIND RIVER MULTIPLE USE ADVOCATES, PO Box 468, Riverton, WY 82501. (307) 856-3699.

WYOMING MINING ASSOCIATION, PO Box 866, Cheyenne, WY 82003. (307) 635-0331. FAX (307) 778-6240.

WYOMING STOCK GROWERS ASSOCIATION, PO Box 206, Cheyenne, WY 82003.

THE END

Editor's Note:

Rawhide Western Publishing is dedicated to the restoration and preservation of citizens' rights and freedoms as defined by the Founding Fathers in the U.S. Constitution and Bill of Rights. These, and only these, are the authorized laws of the land. The **RWP** mission is to serve as a conduit for the truth, to better inform the mainstream American public. We survive on no one's funding but our own. Therefore, we must make a small profit on our quality publications. We are prepared, however, to offer maximum discounts from retail prices on multiple book orders. We encourage every concerned citizen to become an important link in the information chain. You can help spread the word to those who don't already know what's happening to our American way of life. Use the order coupons in the back of this book. Organizations may arrange speaking engagements with our authors through **Rawhide Western Publishing**, PO Box 327, Safford, AZ 85548, or call 1-800-428-5956.

Bibliography

Arnold, Ron and Gottlieb, Alan, *Trashing the Economy: How Runaway Environmentalism Is Wrecking America*, (Bellevue, WA; The Free Enterprise Press, 1993)

Bouvier, John, *A Law Dictionary, Adapted to the Constitution and Laws of the United States of America, and of the Several States of the American Union: with References to the Civil and Other Systems of Foreign Law*, (Boston, MA; Little, Brown & Company, 1880)

Clausen, Barry with Pomeroy, DanaRae, *Walking On the Edge: How I Infiltrated Earth First!*, (Olympia, WA; Washington Contract Loggers Association, 1994)

Pendley, William Perry, *It Takes A Hero: The Grassroots Battle Against Environmental Oppression*, (Bellevue, WA; The Free Enterprise Press, 1994)

Pollot, Mark L., *Grand Theft and Petit Larceny: Property Rights In America*, (San Francisco, CA; Pacific Research Institute for Public Policy, 1993)

Singer, Dr. Sydney, *The Earth Religion: Reawakening the Human Animal*, (Grass Valley, CA; A.B.A.C.E. Publications, 1991)

Walters, Timothy Robert, *Surviving the Second Civil War: The Land Rights Battle . . . and How To Win It*, (Safford, AZ; Rawhide Western Publishing, 1994)

Wolf, Screaming, *A Declaration of War: Killing People To Save Animals and the Environment*, (Grass Valley, CA; Patrick Henry Press, 1991)

Index

Mail This Order to:

Rawhide Western Publishing, PO Box 327, Safford, AZ 85548-0327

___

____copies of *The Endangered American Dream* @ $16.00
____copies of *Surviving the Second Civil War* @ $12.00
_____copies of *From My Cold Dead Fingers* @ $12.00
____copies of *Government, GOD and Freedom* @ $12.00
_____total number of books in this order
_____total price for all books ordered (no shipping added)
Check one:____personal check enclosed____money order
_____cash; or charge my_____VISA____MasterCard
My credit card number is_____
My credit card expiration date is_____
Signature_____
(Please print) Name_____
Address_____
City/State_____
Zipe Code_____Phone(____)_____

___

Fight the Fight—Spread the Word!!!

Use these important titles as gifts to your friends and neighbors . . . or plan a fundraiser for your group or organization. For quantity discounts on any or all titles call 1-800-428-5956. Quality product, personal service and quick delivery!!!
(We accept cash, checks, money orders, MasterCard and Visa. Postal Service or UPS delivery. Sorry, no C.O.D.s)

Knowledge is Power!

We'll Help You Win the Battle.

USE THIS PAGE
FOR EASY DISCOUNT ORDERS
(Reduced Price and No Shipping Charge)

The Endangered American Dream: Land Lock—the Cancer That's Killing America . . . and How To Stop It! By Timothy Robert Walters
Reg. ~~$16.95 plus $3.00 S & H~~...with this page just $16.00!

Surviving the Second Civil War: The Land Rights Battle . . . and How To Win It! By Timothy Robert Walters
Reg. ~~$12.95 plus $2.00 S & H~~...with this page just $12.00!

From My Cold Dead Fingers: Why America Needs Guns, By Richard I. Mack and Timothy Robert Walters
Reg. ~~$12.95 plus $2.00 S & H~~...with this page just $12.00!

Government, GOD and Freedom: A Fundamental Trinity, By Timothy Robert Walters and Richard I. Mack
Reg. ~~$12.95 plus $2.00 S & H~~...with this page just $12.00!

Order Form on Reverse Side

Or Call 1-800-428-5956
for Bigger Savings on Multiple-Copy Orders